CALL ME ISHMAEL

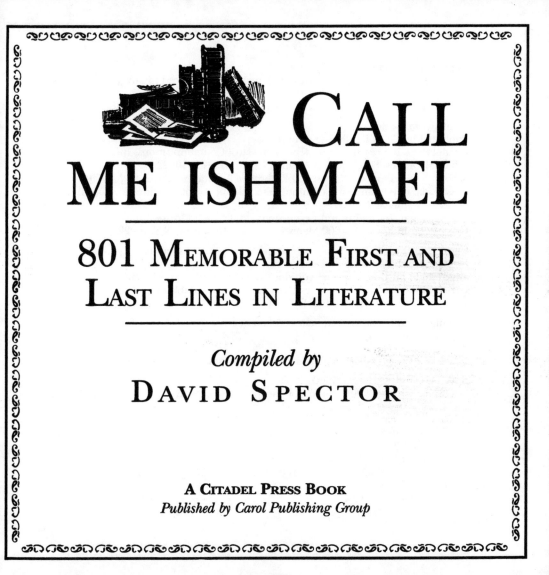

CALL ME ISHMAEL

801 MEMORABLE FIRST AND LAST LINES IN LITERATURE

Compiled by

DAVID SPECTOR

A CITADEL PRESS BOOK
Published by Carol Publishing Group

A Citadel Press Book
Published by Carol Publishing Group
Citadel Press is a registered trademark of Carol Communications, Inc.
Editorial Offices: 600 Madison Avenue, New York, N.Y. 10022
Sales and Distribution Offices: 120 Enterprise Avenue, Secaucus, N.J. 07094
In Canada: Canadian Manda Group, One Atlantic Avenue, Suite 105, Toronto,
    Ontario M6K 3E7
Queries regarding rights and permissions should be addressed to
Carol Publishing Group, 600 Madison Avenue, New York, N.Y. 10022

Carol Publishing Group books are available at special discounts
for bulk purchases, sales promotion, fund-raising, or
educational purposes. Special editions can be created to specifications.
For details, contact: Special Sales Department, Carol Publishing
Group, 120 Enterprise Avenue, Secaucus, N.J. 07094

Manufactured in the United States of America
10   9   8   7   6   5   4   3   2   1

Library of Congress Cataloging-in-Publication Data

Spector, David A. (David Alan), 1934–
    Call me Ishmael : 801 memorable first and last lines in
literature / David A. Spector.
        p.   cm.
    Includes index.
    "A Citadel Press book."
    ISBN 0-8065-1657-7 (pbk.)
    1. Openings (Rhetoric)   2. Closure (Rhetoric)   3. Quotations,
English.   I. Title.
PN6084.063S64   1995
808—dc20   95-19927

To my brother, James.

Keep turning those pages!

Contents

Introduction

❧ ❧ ❧ ❧ ❧ ❧

T<small>HE PRINTED WORD</small> has been with us for nearly six hundred years. Most books have long since been forgotten, but many have endured. What I have gathered here are first or last lines from those that I consider lasting for their powerful insights, their dramatic narrative, their incisive wit, or their linguistic surprises. They run the gamut from Leo Tolstoy to Woody Allen, from the Bible to A. A. Milne.

Some first and last sentences you will find here employ only one word, while others take up a page of text. Many are descriptive, as factual as a ship's log or a police report; still others are incredibly lyrical and moving. Consider this last line from Toni Morrison's novel *Sula*. "It was a fine cry—loud and long—but it had no bottom and it had no top, just circles and circles of sorrow." Other lines are as comfortable and familiar as old friends or cherished customs. The opening sentence of Jane Austen's *Pride and Prejudice* is such an example: "It is a truth universally acknowledged, that a single man in possession of a good fortune must be in want of a wife."

Most of the lines compiled here are classics, some are not, but I found them irresistible. My hope is that, through these sentences, the reader will make new friends, find new books to read, and become more aware of the tremendous diversity of the creative process.

I will leave the last word to the last sentence of Cervantes' great novel *Don Quixote.*

"Farewell."

FIRST LINES

A

Under the shadow of Boston State House, turning its back on the house of John Hancock, the little passage called Hancock Avenue runs, or ran, from Beacon Street, skirting the State House grounds, to Mount Vernon Street, on the summit of Beacon Hill; and there, in the third house below Mount Vernon Place, February 16, 1838, a child was born, and christened later by his uncle, the minister of First Church after the tenets of Boston Unitarianism, as Henry Brooks Adams.

Henry Adams, *The Education of Henry Adams,* **1918**

On the theory that our genuine impulses may be connected with our childish experiences, that one's bent may be tracked back to that "No-Man's Land" where character is formless but nevertheless settling into definite lines of future development, I begin this record with some impressions of my childhood.

Jane Addams, *Twenty Years at Hull-House,* **1910**

A famished fox crept into a vineyard where ripe luscious grapes were draped high over arbors in a most tempting display.

Aesop's Fables, **6TH CENTURY B.C.**
Edited by Jack Zipes, based on Thomas James translation, 1848

Knoxville, Summer, 1915
We are talking now of summer evenings in Knoxville, Tennessee, in the time that I lived there so successfully disguised to myself as a child.

James Agee, *A Death in the Family,* **1957**

"Christmas won't be Christmas without any presents," grumbled Jo, lying on the rug.

Louisa May Alcott, *Little Women,* **1868–69**

The town of the little people into which I shall take you, dear reader, is exactly in the middle of that blessed Pale into which Jews have been packed as closely as herring in a barrel and told to increase and multiply.

Sholom Aleichem, "The Old Country," 1946
Trans. by Julius and Frances Butwin, 1946

One Saturday afternoon in January a lively and animated group of boys were gathered on the western side of a large pond in the village of Groveton.

Horatio Alger Jr., *Struggling Upward; or, Luke Larkin's Luck,* 1890

"He's just a pore lonesome wife-left feller," the more understanding said of Fitz Linkhorn, "losin' his old lady is what crazied him."

Nelson Algren, *A Walk on the Wild Side,* 1956

Getting through the night is becoming harder and harder.

Woody Allen, "Selections From the Allen Notebooks,"
***Without Feathers,* 1972**

It came down to this: if I had not been arrested by the Turkish police, I would have been arrested by the Greek police.

Eric Ambler, *The Light of Day,* **1962**

The writer, an old man with a white mustache, had some difficulty getting into bed.

Sherwood Anderson, "The Book of Grotesque,"
Winesburg, Ohio, **1919**

Kit didn't speak much or often of her father.

Sherwood Anderson, *Kit Brandon,* **1936**

It is related—but God knows and see best what lies hidden in the old accounts of bygone peoples and times—that long ago, during the time of the Sasanid dynasty, in the peninsulas of India and Indochina, there lived two kings who were brothers.

Prologue, *The Arabian Nights,* **9TH CENTURY**
Trans. by Husain Haddawy, 1988

September 10, 1939.
I have always wanted to keep a journal, but whenever I am about to
start one, I am dissuaded by the idea that it is too late.

Louis Auchincloss, *The Rector of Justin,* **1964**

The naked child ran out of the hide-covered lean-to toward the rock
beach at the bend in the small river.

Jean M. Auel, *The Clan of the Cave Bear,* **1980**

It is a truth universally acknowledged, that a single man in possession
of a good fortune must be in want of a wife.

Jane Austen, *Pride and Prejudice,* **1813**

No one who had ever seen Catherine Morland in her infancy, would
have supposed her born to be an heroine.

Jane Austen, *Northanger Abbey,* POSTHUMOUS, **1906**

Everyone had always said that Jon would be a preacher when he grew up, just like his father.

James Baldwin, *Go Tell It on the Mountain*, 1953

I stand at the window of this great house in the south of France as night falls, the night which is leading me to the most terrible morning of my life.

James Baldwin, *Giovanni's Room*, 1956

In some country towns there exist houses whose appearance weighs heavily upon the spirit as the gloomiest cloister, the most dismal ruin, or the dreariest stretch of barren land.

Honoré de Balzac, *Eugenie Grandet*, 1833
Trans. by Marion Ayton Crawford, 1955

This is the story of my older brother's strange criminal behavior and his disappearance.

Russell Banks, *Affliction,* **1989**

All children, except one, grow up.

J. M. Barrie, *Peter Pan* [*Peter Pan and Wendy*], **1911**

"At this point I interrupted my sister as usual to say, 'You have a way with words, Scheherazade.'"

John Barth, *Chimera,* **1972**

Dorothy lived in the midst of the great Kansas prairies, with Uncle Henry, who was a farmer, and Aunt Em, who was the farmer's wife.

L. Frank Baum, *The Wonderful Wizard of Oz,* **1900**

I shall soon be dead at last in spite of all.

Samuel Beckett, *Malone Dies,* **1951**

That old bell, presage of a train, had just sounded through Oxford station; and the undergraduates who were waiting there, gay figures in tweed or flannel, moved to the margin of the platform and gazed idly up the line.

Max Beerbohm, *Zuleika Dobson,* **1911**

I am an American, Chicago born—Chicago, that somber city—and go at things as I have taught myself, free-style, and will make a record in my own way: first to knock, first admitted: sometimes an innocent knock, sometimes a not so innocent.

Saul Bellow, *The Adventures of Augie March,* **1953**

We are to consider these passions termed political, owing to which men rise up against other men, the chief of which are racial passions, class passions and national passions.

Julian Benda, *The Treason of the Intellectuals,* **1927**
Trans. by Richard Aldington, 1928

Hwæt, we gar-dena in ȝear-daȝum
þeod-cyninȝa þrym ȝefrunon,
hu ða æþelinȝas ellen fremedon.

***Beowulf*, CA. 800**

Yes, we have heard of the glory of the Spear-Danes' king in the old days—how the princes of that people did brave deeds.

Trans. by E. Talbot Donaldson, 1975

Now we have heard   stories of high valor
in times past   of tribal monarchs,
lords of Denmark,   how these leaders strove.

Trans. by Ruth P. Lehmann, 1988

I am a white man and never forget it, but I was brought up by the Cheyenne Indians from the age of ten.

Thomas Berger, *Little Big Man*, 1964

Fred Wagner began his career of public invisibility in a large midtown post office.

Thomas Berger, *Being Invisible*, 1987

In the beginning God created the heaven and the earth.

The Bible, King James Version, 1611

In the beginning of the creation, when God made heaven and earth, the earth was without form and void, with darkness over the face of the abyss, and a mighty wind that swept over the surface of the waters.

The New English Bible, 1970

A man stood upon a railroad bridge in northern Alabama, looking down into the swift water twenty feet below.

Ambrose Bierce, "An Occurrence at Owl Creek Bridge," 1891

They were to have met in the garden of the *Chapelle Expiatoire* at five o'clock in the afternoon, but Julio Desnoyers with the impatience of a lover who hopes to advance the moment of meeting by presenting himself before the appointed time, arrived an half hour earlier.

Vicente Blasco Ibáñez, *The Four Horsemen of the Apocalypse*, 1916
Trans. by Charlotte Brewster Jordan, 1918

I owe the discovery of Uqbar to the conjunction of a mirror and an encyclopedia.

Jorge Luis Borges, "Tlön, Uqbar, Orbis Tertius," 1940
Trans. by James E. Irby, 1961

That morning's ice, no more than a brittle film, had cracked and was now floating in segments.

Elizabeth Bowen, *The Death of the Heart*, 1938

He awoke, opened his eyes.

Paul Bowles, *The Sheltering Sky*, 1949

My first act on entering this world was to kill my mother.

William Boyd, *The New Confession*, 1988

He was swimming, rotating from front to back, thrashing his arms and legs and puffing out his cheeks, and it seemed as if he'd been swimming forever.

T. Coraghessan Boyle, *East Is East*, 1990

It was a warm afternoon in early September when I first met the Illustrated Man.

Ray Bradbury, Prologue, *The Illustrated Man*, 1951

It was a pleasure to burn.

Ray Bradbury, *Fahrenheit 451*, 1953

Here's Mother Courage and her wagon!
Hey, Captain, let them come and buy!
Beer by the keg! Wine by the flagon!
Let your men drink before they die!

**Bertolt Brecht, Prologue, *Mother Courage
and Her Children*, 1939**
Trans. by Eric Bentley, 1950

You would never know you were in New York City if you stand on the beach in the late afternoon at Rockaway.

Jimmy Breslin, *World Without End, Amen*, 1973

There was no possibility of taking a walk that day.

Charlotte Brontë, *Jane Eyre*, 1847

1801 — I have just returned from a visit to my landlord—the solitary neighbour that I shall be troubled with.

Emily Brontë, *Wuthering Heights,* **1847**

I thought of her as the aunt rather than as my aunt, for anything more intimate would have implied appropriation or attachment.

Anita Brookner, *Dolly,* **1993**

It began with Christopher Columbus, who gave the people the name *Indios.*

Dee Brown, *Bury My Heart at Wounded Knee,* **1970**

For my religion, though there be several Circumstances that might persuade the World I have none at all, (as the general scandal of my Profession, the natural course of my Studies, the indifference of my Behaviour and Discourse in matters of Religion, neither violently Defending one, nor with that common ardour and contention Opposing another;) yet, in despight hereof, I dare without usurpation assume the honourable Stile of a Christian.

Sir Thomas Browne, *Religio Medici,* **1642**

It was Wang Lung's marriage day.

Pearl S. Buck, *The Good Earth,* **1931**

At the hour of sunset, on a hot spring day, two citizens appeared in the Patriarchs' Ponds Park.

Mikhail Bulgakov, *The Master and Margarita,* **POSTHUMOUS, 1966**
Trans. by Mirra Ginsburg, 1967

"Ho, Diomed, well met! Do you sup with Glaucus tonight?" said a young man of small stature, who wore his tunic in those loose and effeminate folds which proved him a gentleman and a coxcomb.

Edward George Bulwer-Lytton, *The Last Days of Pompeii,* **1834**

As I walk'd through the wilderness of this world, I lighted on a certain place where was a Den; and I laid me down in that place to sleep: and as I slept, I dreamed a Dream.

John Bunyan, *The Pilgrim's Progress From This World to That Which Is to Come,* **PART 1, 1678**

"What's it going to be then, eh?"

Anthony Burgess, *A Clockwork Orange,* **1962**

It was the afternoon of my eighty-first birthday, and I was in bed with my catamite when Ali announced that the archbishop had come to see me.

Anthony Burgess, *Earthly Powers*, 1980

Cedric himself knew nothing whatever about it.

Frances Hodgson Burnett, *Little Lord Fauntleroy*, 1886

When Mary Lennox was sent to Misselthwaite Manor to live with her uncle, everybody said she was the most disagreeable-looking child ever seen.

Frances Hodgson Burnett, *The Secret Garden*, 1911

I had this story from one who had no business to tell it to me, or to any other.

Edgar Rice Burroughs, *Tarzan of the Apes*, 1914

When I was a small boy at the beginning of the century I remember an old man who wore knee-breeches and worsted stockings, and who used to hobble about the streets of our village with the aid of a stick.

Samuel Butler, *The Way of All Flesh*, POSTHUMOUS, 1903

The whole of Gaul is divided into three parts; of these one is inhabited by the Belgae, a second by the Aquitani, and the third by a people called Celts in their own language and Gauls in ours.

Julius Caesar, *The Gallic War*, CA. 58–44 B.C.
Trans. by Moses Hadas, 1957

They threw me off the hay truck about noon.

James M. Cain, *The Postman Always Rings Twice*, 1934

Several yards of undetermined sand and clay broke loose up near the top, and the land slid down to the floor of the crater.

Erskine Caldwell, *God's Little Acre*, 1933

Mother died today.

Albert Camus, *The Stranger*, 1942
Trans. by Stuart Gilbert, 1946

"What are you doing here, my little man?"
Elias Canetti, *Auto-da-Fé*, 1935
Trans. by C. V. Wedgwood, 1966

If you were to look for the little island of Tanah Masa on the map, you would find it right on the equator, a bit to the west of Sumatra; but if on board the ship *Kandong Bandoeng* you were to ask Captain J. van Toch what is this Tanah Masa before which he has just dropped anchor, he would curse for a while, and then tell you that it is the dirtiest hole in all the Straits, even worse than Tanah Bala and at least as damned as Pini, or Banjak; that the only—I beg your pardon—man who lives there—not counting, of course, those lousy Bataks—is a drunken commercial agent, a cross between a Cuban and a Portuguese, and a bigger thief, heathen and swine than a pure Cuban and a pure white man put together; and if there is anything damned in this world, then it is the damned life on this damned Tanah Masa, sir.

Karel Čapek, *The War With the Newts*, 1936
Trans. by M. and R. Weatherall, 1937

Now a traveler must make his way to Noon City by the best means he can, for there are no buses or trains heading in that direction, though six days a week a truck from the Chuberry Turpentine Company collects mail and supplies in the next-door town of Paradise Chapel:

occasionally a person bound for Noon City can catch a ride with the driver of the truck, Sam Radclif.

Truman Capote, *Other Voices, Other Rooms*, 1948

I am always drawn back to places where I have lived, the houses and their neighborhoods.

Truman Capote, *Breakfast at Tiffany's*, 1958

At the age of twenty-four, I was more prepared for death than I was for life.

Philip Caputo, *A Rumor of War*, 1977

Alice was beginning to get very tired of sitting by her sister on the bank, and having nothing to do: once or twice she had peeped into the book her sister was reading, but it had no pictures or conversations in it, "and what is the use of a book," thought Alice, "without pictures or conversations?"

Lewis Carroll, *Alice's Adventures in Wonderland*, 1865

I remember how, that night, I lay awake in the wagon-lit in a tender, delicious ecstasy of excitement, my burning cheek pressed against the impeccable linen of the pillow and the pounding of my heart mimicking that of the great pistons ceaselessly thrusting the train that bore me through the night, away from Paris, away from girlhood, away from the white, enclosed quietude of my mother's apartment, into the unguessable country of marriage.

Angela Carter, "The Bloody Chamber," 1979

The Rev. Mr. Tyson, having been sentenced to six months in gaol, had his eye cut by a broken bottle as they tried to smuggle him out of court by a back way.

Joyce Cary, *The Captive and the Free*, 1959

In the year 1428 Don Jacobe Casanova, born at Saragossa, the capital of Aragon, natural son of Don Francisco, abducted Donna Anna Palafox from a convent on the day after she had taken her vows.

Jacques Casanova, *History of My Life*, 1966
Trans. by Willard Trask, 1966

I first heard of Ántonia on what seemed to me an interminable journey across the great midland plain of North America.

Willa Cather, *My Ántonia*, 1918

Here we are, alone again.

Louis-Ferdinand Céline, *Death on the Installment Plan,* **1936**
Trans. by Ralph Manheim, 1966

All men of every sort, who have done anything that is meritorious, or that indeed resembles merit, ought, if they be truthful persons and of good report, to set forth their lives with their own hand; but they should not commence so noble an undertaking before they have passed the age of forty years.

Benvenuto Cellini, *The Autobiography of Benvenuto Cellini,*
POSTHUMOUS, 1730 [CA. 1559]
Trans. by Robert Hobart, 1961

In a certain village in La Mancha, which I do not wish to name, there lived not long ago a gentleman—one of those who have always a lance in the rack, an ancient shield, a lean hack and a greyhound for coursing.

Miguel de Cervantes, *Don Quixote,* **1605**
Trans. by J. M. Cohen, 1950

It was about eleven o'clock in the morning, mid October, with the sun not shining and a look of hard wet rain in the clearness of the foothills.

Raymond Chandler, *The Big Sleep,* **1939**

When that Aprille with his shoures soote
The droghte of March hath perced to the roote,
And bathed every veyne in swich licour
Of which vertu engendred is the flour;
When Zephirus eek with his sweete breeth
Inspired hath in every holt and heeth
The tendre croppes, and the yonge sonne
Hath in the Ram his halfe courss yronne,
And smale foweles maken melodye,
That slepen al the nyght with open ye
(So priketh hem nature in hir corages);
Thanne longen folk to goon on pilgrimages,
To ferne halwes, kouthe in sondry londes;
And specially, from every shires ende
Of Engelond, to Caunterbury they wende,
The hooly blisful martir for to seke
That hem hath holpen when that they were seke.

When April with his sweet showers has
pierced the drought of March to the root,
and bathed every vein in such moisture
as has power to bring forth the flower;
when, also, Zephyrus with his sweet breath
has breathed spirit into the tender new shoots
in every wood and meadow, and the young sun
has run half his course in the sign of the Ram,

and small birds sing melodies and
sleep with their eyes open all the night
(so Nature pricks them in their hearts):
then people long to go on pilgrimages,
and palmers long to seek strange shores
and far-off shires known in various lands,
and especially, from the ends of every shire
in England they come to Canterbury,
to seek the holy, blissful martyr
who helped them when they were sick.

Geoffrey Chaucer, General Prologue, *The Canterbury Tales,*
1387–1394

The snow began to fall into St. Botolphs at four-fifteen on
Christmas Eve.

John Cheever, *The Wapshot Scandal,* **1964**

The suburb of Saffron Park lay on the sunset side of London, as red
and ragged as a cloud of sunset.

G. K. Chesterton, *The Man Who Was Thursday,* **1908**

Harold March, the rising reviewer and social critic, was walking vigorously across a great table-land of moors and commons, the horizon of which was fringed with the far-off woods of the famous estate of Torwood Park.

G. K. Chesterton, *The Man Who Knew Too Much,* **1922**

Captain Crosbie came out of the bank with the pleased air of one who has cashed a cheque and has discovered that there is just a little more in his account than he thought there was.

Agatha Christie, *They Came to Baghdad,* **1951**

After the end of the World War of 1914 there was a deep conviction and almost universal hope that peace would reign in the world.

Winston S. Churchill, *The Gathering Storm,* **1948**

Gil and I crossed the eastern divide about two by the sun.

Walter Van Tilburg Clark, *The Ox-Bow Incident,* **1940**

Towards ten o'clock, the family poker-players began to show signs of weariness.

Colette, *The Cat,* **1933**
Trans. by Antonia White, 1953

This is the story of what a Woman's patience can endure, and what a Man's resolution can achieve.

Wilkie Collins, *The Woman in White,* **1860**

My wife is precise, elegant, and well-dressed, but the sloppiness of my mistress knows few bounds.

Laurie Colwin, "My Mistress," *Another Marvelous Thing,* **1986**

Often he thought: My life did not begin until I knew her.

Evan S. Connell, *Mr. Bridge,* **1969**

The more books we read, the sooner we perceive that the true function of a writer is to produce a masterpiece and that no other task is of any consequence.

Cyril Connolly, *The Unquiet Grave,* **1944**

In 1920 I was a schoolboy; in 1930 I got married.

Cyril Connolly, *The Evening Colonnade,* **1973**

He was an inch, perhaps two, under six feet, powerfully built, and he advanced straight at you with a slight stoop of the shoulders, head forward, and a fixed from-under stare which made you think of a charging bull.

Joseph Conrad, *Lord Jim,* **1900**

It was a feature peculiar to the Colonial wars of North America, that the toils and dangers of the wilderness were to be encountered before the adverse hosts could meet.

James Fenimore Cooper, *The Last of the Mohicans,* **1826**

I have been young and now am old.

James Gould Cozzens, *Morning, Noon, and Night,* **1968**

The cold passed reluctantly from the earth, and the retiring fogs revealed an army stretched out on the hills, resting.

Stephen Crane, *The Red Badge of Courage,* **1895**

As the public seem to feel some interest in the history of an individual so humble as I am, and as that history can be so well known to no person living as to myself, I have, after so long a time, and under many pressing solicitations from my friends and acquaintances, at last determined to put my own hand to it, and lay before the world a narrative on which they may at least rely as being true.

David Crockett, *A Narrative of the Life of David Crockett,* **1834**

Late one October afternoon in the year 1921, a shabby young man gazed with fixed intensity through the window of a third-class compartment in the almost empty train labouring up the Penowell valley from Swansea.

A. J. Cronin, *The Citadel,* **1937**

The fourteenth of August was the day fixed upon for the sailing of the brig *Pilgrim*, on her voyage from Boston, round Cape Horn, to the western coast of North America.

Richard Henry Dana Jr., *Two Years Before the Mast,* **1840**

In the middle of the journey of our life I came to myself in a dark wood where the straight way was lost.

Dante Alighieri, "Hell," *The Divine Comedy,* CA. **1300-15**
Trans. by John Aitken Carlyle, Thomas Okey, and P. H. Wicksteed, 1950

When we compare the individuals of the same variety or sub-variety of our older cultivated plants and animals, one of the first points which strikes us is, that they generally differ more from each other than do the individuals of any one species or variety in a state of nature.

Charles Darwin, *Origin of Species by Means of Natural Selection or the Preservation of Favoured Races in the Struggle for Life,* **1859**

Once in a long while, as a great treat, Father took me down to his office.

Clarence Day, *Life With Father,* 1935

I was born in the Year 1632, in the city of *York,* of a good Family, tho' not of that country, my Father being a Foreigner, of *Bremen,* who settled first at *Hull:* He got a good Estate by Merchandise, and leaving off his Trade, lived afterward at *York,* from whence he had married my Mother, whose Relations were named *Robinson,* a very good Family in that Country and from whom I was called *Robinson Kreutznaer;* but by the usual Corruption of Words in *England,* we are now called, nay we call ourselves, and write our Name *Crusoe,* and so my Companions always call'd me.

Daniel Defoe, *Robinson Crusoe,* 1719–20

It has rained all day.

Patrick Dennis, *Auntie Mame,* 1955

In the spring of that year, an epidemic of rabies broke out in Ether County, Georgia.

Pete Dexter, *Paris Trout,* 1988

The first ray of light which illumines the gloom, and converts into a dazzling brilliancy that obscurity in which the earliest history of the public career of the immortal Pickwick would appear to be involved, is derived from the perusal of the following entry in the Transactions of the Pickwick Club, which the editor of these papers feels the highest pleasure in laying before his readers, as a proof of the careful attention, indefatigable assiduity, and nice discrimination, with which his search among the multifarious documents confided to him has been conducted.

Charles Dickens, *The Pickwick Papers,* 1836–37

Whether I shall turn out to be the hero of my own life, or whether that station will be held by anybody else, these pages must show.

Charles Dickens, *David Copperfield,* 1849–50

It was the best of times, it was the worst of times, it was the age of wisdom, it was the age of foolishness, it was the epoch of belief, it was the epoch of incredulity, it was the season of Light, it was the season of Darkness, it was the spring of hope, it was the winter of despair, we had everything before us, we had nothing before us, we were all going direct to Heaven, we were all going direct the other way—in short, the period was so far like the present period, that some of its noisiest authorities insisted on its being received, for good or for evil in the superlative degree of comparison only.

Charles Dickens, *A Tale of Two Cities*, 1859

I had a farm in Africa, at the foot of the Ngong Hills.

Isak Dinesen, *Out of Africa*, 1937

"I remember him as a little boy," said the Duchess, "a pretty little boy, but very shy."

Benjamin Disraeli, *Lothair*, 1870

On a bright December morning long ago, two thinly clad children were kneeling upon the bank of a frozen canal in Holland.

Mary Mapes Dodge, *Hans Brinker; or, The Silver Skates*, 1865

On an exceptionally hot evening early in July a young man came out of the garret in which he lodged in S. Place and walked slowly, as though in hesitation, towards K. Bridge.

Fyodor Dostoyevsky, *Crime and Punishment*, 1866
Trans. by Constance Garnett, 1934

At nine o'clock in the morning, towards the end of November, the Warsaw train was approaching Petersburg at full speed.

Fyodor Dostoyevsky, *The Idiot,* **1868**
Trans. by Constance Garnett, 1934

Alexey Fyodorovich Karamazov was the third son of Fyodor Pavlovich Karamazov, a landowner well known in our district in his own day (and still remembered among us) owing to his tragic and obscure death, which happened exactly thirteen years ago, and which I shall describe in its proper place.

Fyodor Dostoyevsky, *The Brothers Karamazov,* **1879–80**
Trans. by Constance Garnett, rev. by Ralph E. Matlaw, 1976

In the year 1878 I took my degree of Doctor of Medicine of the University of London, and proceeded to Netley to go through the course prescribed for surgeons in the army.

Sir Arthur Conan Doyle, *A Study in Scarlet,* **1887**

When Frank Algernon Cowperwood emerged from the Eastern District Penitentiary in Philadelphia he realized that the old life he had lived in that city since boyhood was ended.

Theodore Dreiser, *The Titan,* **1914**

Dusk—of a summer night.

Theodore Dreiser, *An American Tragedy,* **1925**

Last night I dreamt I went to Manderley again.

Daphne du Maurier, *Rebecca,* **1938**

On February 24, 1815, the watchtower at Marseilles signaled the arrival of the three-master *Pharaon,* coming from Smyrna, Trieste and Naples.

Alexandre Dumas, *The Count of Monte Cristo,* **1844**
Trans. by Lowell Bair, 1956

"When your mama was the geek, my dreamlets," Papa would say, "she made the nipping off of noggins such a crystal mystery that the hens themselves yearned toward her, waltzing around her, hypnotized with longing. 'Spread your lips, sweet Lil,' they'd cluck, 'and show us your choppers!'"

Katherine Dunn, *Geek Love,* **1989**

One day, I was already old, in the entrance of a public place a man came up to me.

Marguerite Duras, *The Lover,* **1984**
Trans. by Barbara Bray, 1985

The sea is high again today, with a thrilling flush of wind.

Lawrence Durrell, *Justine,* **1957**

In the beginning was the Word and the Word was with God, and the Word was God.

Umberto Eco, *The Name of the Rose*, 1980
Trans. by William Weaver, 1983

That was when I saw the Pendulum.

Umberto Eco, *Foucault's Pendulum*, 1988
Trans. by William Weaver, 1989

A wide plain, where the broadening Floss hurries on between its green banks to the sea, and the loving tide, rushing to meet it, checks its passage with an impetuous embrace.

George Eliot, *The Mill on the Floss*, 1860

In the days when the spinning-wheel hummed busily in the farmhouses—and even great ladies, clothed in silk and thread-lace, had their toy spinning-wheels of polished oak—there might be seen in districts far away among the lanes, or deep in the bosom of the hills, certain pallid undersized men, who, by the side of the brawny, country-folk, looked like the remnants of a disinherited race.

George Eliot, *Silas Marner 1861*

I am an invisible man.

Ralph Ellison, *Invisible Man,* **1952**

In the winter of 1918–1919, on a day when the wind was blowing, I. C. Trumpelman arrived in our town.

Leslie Epstein, *King of the Jews,* **1979**

Polydorus:
Back from the pit of the dead,
from the somber door
that opens into hell, where no god goes, I have come,
     the ghost of Polydorus,
son and last surviving heir of Hecuba
and Priam, king of Troy.

    Euripides, *Hecuba,* **CA. 424 B.C.**
    Trans. by William Arrowsmith, 1956

Studs Lonigan, on the verge of fifteen, and wearing his first suit of long trousers, stood in the bathroom with a Sweet Caporal pasted in his mug.

James T. Farrell, *Young Lonigan,* **1932**

On a cool, pleasant early fall morning, in the year 1774, Dr. Benjamin Franklin was told that Thomas Paine had been waiting to see him for almost an hour.

Howard Fast, *Citizen Tom Paine,* **1943**

Jewel and I come up from the field, following the path in single file.

William Faulkner, *As I Lay Dying,* **1930**

From beyond the screen of bushes which surrounded the spring, Popeye watched the man drinking.

William Faulkner, *Sanctuary,* **1931**

Sitting beside the the road, watching the wagon mount the hill toward her, Lena thinks, "I have come from Alabama: a fur piece."

William Faulkner, *Light in August,* **1932**

The jury said "Guilty" and the Judge said "Life" but he didn't hear them.

William Faulkner, *The Mansion,* **1960**

Bizarre as was the name she bore, Kim Ravenal always said she was thankful it had been no worse.

Edna Ferber, *Show Boat,* **1926**

It is a trite but true Observation, that Examples work more forcibly on the mind than Precepts: And if this be just in what is odious and blameable, it is more strongly so in what is amiable and praise-worthy.

Henry Fielding, *Joseph Andrews,* **1742**

An Author ought to consider himself, not as a Gentleman who gives a private or eleemosynary Treat, but rather as one who keeps a public Ordinary, at which all Persons are welcome for their Money.

Henry Fielding, *Tom Jones,* **1749**

In shirt-sleeves, the way I generally worked, I sat sketching a bar of soap taped to an upper corner of my drawing board.

Jack Finney, *Time and Again,* **1970**

Amory Blaine inherited from his mother every trait, except the stray inexpressible few, that made him worth while.

F. Scott Fitzgerald, *This Side of Paradise,* **1920**

In my younger and more vulnerable years my father gave me some advice that I've been turning over in my mind ever since.

F. Scott Fitzgerald, *The Great Gatsby,* **1925**

Though I haven't ever been on the screen I was brought up in pictures.

F. Scott Fitzgerald, *The Last Tycoon,* **1941**

We were in study hall when the headmaster walked in, followed by a new boy not wearing a school uniform, and by a janitor carrying a large desk.

Gustave Flaubert, *Madame Bovary,* **1856**
Trans. by Lowell Bair, 1959

James Bond, with two double bourbons inside him, sat in the final departure lounge of Miami Airport and thought about life and death.

Ian Fleming, *Goldfinger,* 1959

This is the saddest story I have ever heard.

Ford Madox Ford, *The Good Soldier,* 1915

One may as well begin with Helen's letters to her sister.

E. M. Forster, *Howards End,* 1910

Except for the Marabar Caves—and they are twenty miles off—the city of Chandrapore presents nothing extraordinary.

E. M. Forster, *A Passage to India,* 1924

I was born in 1927, the only child of middle-class parents, both English, and themselves born in the grotesquely elongated shadow, which they never rose sufficiently above history to leave, of that monstrous dwarf Queen Victoria.

John Fowles, *The Magus,* 1965

An easterly is the most disagreeable wind in Lyme Bay—Lyme Bay being that largest bite from the underside of England's outstretched southwestern leg—and a person of curiosity could at once have deduced several strong probabilities about the pair who began to walk down the quay at Lyme Regis, the small but ancient eponym of the inbite, one incisively sharp and blustery morning in the late March of 1867.

John Fowles, *The French Lieutenant's Woman,* **1969**

I told the boys to stay quiet while I went to fetch my gun.

Dick Francis, *Twice Shy,* **1982**

To deny a people the man whom it praises as the greatest of its sons is not a deed to be undertaken lightheartedly—especially by one belonging to that people.

Sigmund Freud, *Moses and Monotheism,* **1939**
Trans. by Katherine Jones, 1939

Incredible the first animal that dreamed of another animal.

Carlos Fuentes, *Terra Nostra,* **1975**
Trans. by Margaret Sayers Peden, 1976

My friend's pallor was not unusual.

Carlos Fuentes, *Distant Relations,* **1980**
Trans. by Margaret Sayers Peden, 1982

Wealth is not without its advantages and the case to the contrary, although it has often been made, has never proved widely persuasive.

John Kenneth Galbraith, *The Affluent Society,* **1958**

Those privileged to be present at a family festival of the Forsytes have seen that charming and instructive sight—an upper middle-class family in full plumage.

John Galsworthy, *The Man of Property,* **first volume in** *The Forsyte Saga,* **1906**

Many years later, as he faced the firing squad, Colonel Aureliano Buendía was to remember that distant afternoon when his father took him to discover ice.

Gabriel García Márquez, *One Hundred Years of Solitude,* **1967**
Trans. by Gregory Rabassa, 1970

It was inevitable: the scent of bitter almonds always reminded him of the fate of unrequited love.

Gabriel García Márquez, *Love in the Time of Cholera,* **1985**
Trans. by Edith Grossman, 1988

Weidmann appeared before you in a five o'clock edition, his head swathed in white bands, a nun and yet a wounded pilot fallen into the rye one September day like the day when the world came to know the name of Our Lady of the Flowers.

Jean Genet, *Our Lady of the Flowers,* **1943**
Trans. by Bernard Frechtman, 1963

In the second century of the Christian era the empire of Rome comprehended the fairest part of the earth and the most civilized portion of mankind.

Edward Gibbon, *The History of the Decline and Fall of the Roman Empire,* **1776–88**

My dear friends, I know you were faithful.

André Gide, *The Immoralist,* **1902**
Trans. by Richard Howard, 1970

Dad was a tall man, with a large head, jowls, and a Herbert Hoover collar.

Frank B. Gilbreth Jr. and Ernestine Gilbreth Carey,
Cheaper by the Dozen, **1948**

The one who saw the abyss I will make the land know;
Of him who knew all, let me tell the whole story
. . . in the same way . . .
[as] the lord of wisdom, he who knew everything, Gilgamesh,
who saw things secret, opened the place hidden,
and carried back word of the time before the Flood—
he travelled the road, exhausted, in pain,
and cut his works into a stone tablet.

Gilgamesh, **CA. 2000 B.C.**
Trans. by John Gardner and John Mair, with Richard A. Henshaw, 1984

For more than a week my pen has lain untouched.

George Gissing, *The Private Papers of Henry Ryecroft,* **1903**

Something very peculiar happened today.

Nikolai Gogol, "The Diary of a Madman," 1835
Trans. by Ronald Wilks, 1972

The boy with fair hair lowered himself down the last few feet of rock and began to pick his way toward the lagoon.

William Golding, *Lord of the Flies,* **1955**

I was ever of the opinion that the honest man who married and brought up a large family did more service than he who continued single and only talked of population.

Oliver Goldsmith, *The Vicar of Wakefield,* **1766**

On the floor, under the window, in a small, shuttered room, lay my father, dressed in a long white garment I had never seen him in before.

Maksim Gorky, "My Childhood," in *Autobiography of My Life,* **1916**
Trans. by Isidor Schneider, 1949

The Mole had been working very hard all morning, spring cleaning his little home.

Kenneth Grahame, *The Wind in the Willows,* **1908**

My family is American, and has been for generations, in all its branches, direct and collateral.

Ulysses S. Grant, *Personal Memoirs of U. S. Grant,* **1892**

Granted: I am an inmate of a mental hospital; my keeper is watching me, he never lets me out of his sight; there's a peep-hole in the door, and my keeper's eye is the shade of brown that can never see through a blue-eyed type like me.

Günter Grass, *The Tin Drum,* **1959**
Trans. by Ralph Manheim, 1962

You tell.

Günter Grass, *Dog Years,* **1963**
Trans. by Ralph Manheim, 1965

I, Tiberius Claudius Druses Nero Germanicus This-that-and-the-other (for I shall not trouble you yet with all my titles) who was once, and not so long ago either, known to my friends and relatives and associates as "Claudius the Idiot," or "That Claudius," or "Claudius the Stammerer," or "Clau-Clau-Claudius" or at best as "Poor Uncle Claudius," am now about to write this strange history of my life; starting from my earliest childhood and continuing year by year until I reach the fateful point of change where, some eight years ago, at the age of fifty-one, I suddenly found myself caught in what I may call the "golden predicament" from which I have never since become disentangled.

Robert Graves, *I, Claudius,* **1934**

There was something about a fête which drew Arthur Rowe irresistibly, bound him a helpless victim to the distant blare of a band and the knock-knock of wooden balls against coconuts.

Graham Greene, *The Ministry of Fear,* **1943**

The cabin-passenger wrote in his diary a parody of Descartes: "I feel discomfort, therefore I am alive," then sat pen in hand with no more to record.

Graham Greene, *A Burnt-Out Case,* **1960**

A sharp clip-clop of iron-shod hoofs deadened and died away, and clouds of yellow dust drifted from under the cottonwoods out over the sage.

Zane Grey, *Riders of the Purple Sage,* **1912**

In olden times, when wishful thinking still helped, there lived a king whose daughters were all beautiful, but the youngest was so beautiful that the sun itself, which had seen so many things, was always filled with amazement each time it cast its rays upon her face.

Brothers Grimm, "The Frog King," *The Complete Fairy Tales of the Brothers Grimm,* **1812–15**
Trans. by Jack Zipes, 1987

My life began on the 1st of May, 1908, and between one thing and another, it still goes on.

Giovanni Guareschi, *The Little World of Don Camillo,* **1950**
Trans. by Una Vincenzo Troubridge, 1950

It is a curious thing that at my age—fifty-five last birthday—I should find myself taking up a pen to try and write history.

H. Rider Haggard, *King Solomon's Mines,* **1885**

After an unequivocal experience of the inefficacy of the subsisting federal government, you are called upon to deliberate on a new Constitution for the United States of America.

Alexander Hamilton, *The Federalist Papers,* **No. 1, October 27, 1787**

The Greeks did not believe that the gods created the universe.

Edith Hamilton, *Mythology,* **1940**

Samuel Spade's jaw was long and bony, his chin a jutting V under the more flexible V of his mouth.

Dashiell Hammett, *The Maltese Falcon,* **1930**

All of this happened while I was walking around starving in Christiania—that strange city no one escapes from until it has left its mark on him. . . .

Knut Hamsun, *Hunger,* **1890**
Trans. by Robert Bly, 1967

A Saturday afternoon in November was approaching the time of twilight, and the vast tract of unenclosed wild known as Egdon Heath embrowned itself moment by moment.

Thomas Hardy, *The Return of the Native,* **1878**

One evening of late summer, before the nineteenth century had reached one-third of its span, a young man and woman, the latter carrying a child, were approaching the large village of Weydon-Priors, in Upper Wessex, on foot.

Thomas Hardy, *The Mayor of Casterbridge,* **1886**

As Mr. John Oakhurst, gambler, stepped into the main street of Poker Flat on the morning of the twenty-third of November 1850, he was conscious of a change in its moral atmosphere since the preceding night.

Bret Harte, "The Outcasts of Poker Flat," 1869

The past is a foreign country: they do things differently there.

L. P. Hartley, *The Go-Between,* **1953**

And so they've killed our Ferdinand, said the charwoman to Mr. Svejk, who had left military service years before, after having been finally certified by an army medical board as an imbecile, and now lived by selling dogs—ugly, mongrel, monstrosities whose pedigrees he forged.

Jaroslav Hašek, *The Good Soldier Švejk,* **1921–23**
Trans. by Cecil Parrott, 1973

A throng of bearded men, in sad-colored garments and gray, steeple-crowned hats, intermixed with women, some wearing hoods, and others bareheaded, was assembled in front of a wooden edifice, the door of which was heavily timbered with oak, and studded with iron spikes.

Nathaniel Hawthorne, *The Scarlet Letter,* **1850**

Half-way down a by-street of one of our New England towns, stands a rusty wooden house, with seven acutely peaked gables facing towards various points of the compass, and a huge clustered chimney in the midst.

Nathaniel Hawthorne, *The House of the Seven Gables,* **1851**

There were fourteen officers on the *Reluctant* and all of them were Reserves.

Thomas Heggen, *Mister Roberts*, 1946

"We need you to kill a man."

Robert A. Heinlein, *The Cat Who Walks Through Walls*, 1985

It was love at first sight.

Joseph Heller, *Catch-22*, 1961

I get the willies when I see closed doors.

Joseph Heller, *Something Happened*, 1974

Robert Cohn was once middleweight boxing champion of Princeton.

Ernest Hemingway, *The Sun Also Rises*, 1926

In the late summer of that year we lived in a house in a village that looked across the river and the plain to the mountains.

Ernest Hemingway, *A Farewell to Arms*, 1929

He lay flat on the brown, pine-needled floor of the forest, his chin on his folded arms, and high overhead the wind blew in the tops of the pine trees.

Ernest Hemingway, *For Whom the Bell Tolls,* **1940**

He was an old man who fished alone in a skiff in the Gulf Stream and he had gone eighty-four days now without taking a fish.

Ernest Hemingway, *The Old Man and the Sea,* **1952**

Herodotus of Halicarnassus, his *Researches* are here set down to preserve the memory of the past by putting on record the astonishing achievements both of our own and of other peoples; and more particularly, to show how they came into conflict.

Herodotus, *The Histories,* CA. **446** B.C.
Trans. by Aubrey de Sélincourt, 1954

As I crawled into bed and put my arm around Helen it occurred to me, not for the first time, that there are few pleasures in this world to compare with snuggling up to a nice woman when you are half frozen.

James Herriot, *All Things Bright and Beautiful,* **1974**

Invasion had come to the town of Adano.
   John Hersey, *A Bell for Adano*, 1944

At exactly fifteen minutes past eight in the morning, on August 6, 1945, Japanese time, at the moment when the atomic bomb flashed on Hiroshima, Miss Toshiko Sasaki, a clerk in the personnel department of the East Asia Tin Works, had just sat down at her place in the patent office and was turning her head to speak to the girl at the next desk.
   John Hersey, *Hiroshima*, 1946

The day had gone by just as days go by.
   Hermann Hesse, *Steppenwolf*, 1927
   Trans. by Basil Creighton, 1929

Once in a while you find yourself in an odd situation.
   Thor Heyerdahl, *Kon Tiki*, 1950
   Trans. by F. H. Lyon, 1950

Someone was digging a grave in one corner of the cemetery as I went in through the lychgate.

Jack Higgins, *The Eagle Has Landed,* **1975**

Cigars had burned low, and we were beginning to sample the disillusionment that usually afflicts old school friends who have met again as men and found themselves with less in common than they had believed they had.

James Hilton, *Lost Horizon,* **1933**

Achilles' baneful wrath resound, O Goddesse, that imposd
Infinite sorrowes on the Greekes, and many brave soules losd
From breast Heroique—sent them farre, to that invisible cave
That no light comforts; and their lims to dogs and vultures gave.

Homer, *The Iliad,* CA. 9TH CENTURY B.C.
Trans. by George Chapman, completed 1611

Anger be now our song, immortal one,
Akhilleus' anger, doomed and ruinous,
that caused the Akhaians loss on bitter loss
and crowded brave souls into the undergloom,
leaving so many dead men—carrion
for dogs and birds; and the will of Zeus was done.

Trans. by Robert Fitzgerald, 1974

The Man, O Muse, informe, that many a way
Wound with his wisdome to his wished stay;
That wandered wondrous farre when He the towne
Of sacred Troy had sackt and shiverd downe.

Homer, *The Odyssey*, CA. 9TH CENTURY B.C.
Trans. by George Chapman, completed 1616

The man for wisdom's various arts renown'd,
Long exercised in woes, O Muse! resound;
Who, when his arms had wrought the destined fall
Of sacred Troy, and razed her heaven-built wall,
Wandering from clime to clime, observant strayed,
Their manners noted, and then states survey'd.

Trans. by Alexander Pope, 1726

Just three hundred forty-eight years, six months, and nineteen days ago today Parisians woke to the sound of bells peeling out within the triple precinct of City, University, and Town.

Victor Hugo, *Notre-Dame de Paris,* **1831**
Trans. by Alban Krailsheimer, 1993

Ships at a distance have every man's wish on board.

Zora Neale Hurston, *Their Eyes Were Watching God,* **1937**

"You won't be late?" There was anxiety in Marjorie Carling's voice, there was something like entreaty.

Aldous Huxley, *Point Counter Point,* **1928**

"The barometer of his emotional nature was set for a spell of riot."
Charles Jackson, *The Lost Weekend*, **1944**

Without, the night was cold and wet, but in the small parlor of Lakesnam Villa the blinds were drawn and the fire burned brightly.
W. W. Jacobs, "The Monkey's Paw," 1902

On a brilliant day in May, in the year 1868, a gentleman was reclining at his ease on the great circular divan which at that period occupied the centre of the Salon Carré, in the Museum of the Louvre.
Henry James, *The American*, **1877**

The story had held us, round the fire, sufficiently breathless, but except the obvious remark that it was gruesome, as on Christmas Eve in old house a strange tale should essentially be, I remember no comment uttered till somebody happened to note it as the only case he had met in which such a visitation had fallen on a child.

Henry James, "The Turn of the Screw," 1898

Ye who listen with credulity to the whispers of fancy, and pursue with eagerness the phantoms of hope who expect that age will perform the promises of youth, and that the deficiencies of the present day will be supplied by the morrow attend to the history of Rasselas, Prince of Abyssinia.

Dr. Samuel Johnson, *The History of Rasselas, Prince of Abyssinia*, 1759

When he finished packing, he walked out on to the third-floor porch of the barracks brushing the dust from his hands, a very neat and deceptively slim young man in the summer khakis that were still early morning fresh.

James Jones, *From Here to Eternity*, 1951

There were 117 psychoanalysts on the Pan Am flight to Vienna and I'd been treated by at least six of them.

Erica Jong, *Fear of Flying*, 1973

Those who essay to write history are actuated, I observe, not by one and the same aim, but by many widely different motives.

Josephus, *Antiquities of the Jews,* A.D. **93**
Trans. by H. St. J. Thackeray, 1930

Once upon a time and a very good time it was there was a moocow coming down along the road and this moocow that was down along the road met a nicens little boy named baby tuckoo. . . .

James Joyce, *Portrait of the Artist as a Young Man,* **1916**

Stately, plump Buck Mulligan came from the stairhead, bearing a bowl of lather on which a mirror and a razor lay crossed.

James Joyce, *Ulysses,* **1922**

riverrun, past Eve and Adam's, from swerve of shore to bend of bay, brings us by a commodius vicus of recirculation back to Howth Castle and Environs.

James Joyce, *Finnegans Wake,* **1939**

As Gregor Samsa awoke one morning from uneasy dreams he found himself transformed in his bed into a gigantic insect.

Franz Kafka, "The Metamorphosis," 1915
Trans. by Willa and Edwin Muir, 1937

Someone must have been telling lies about Joseph K., for without having done anything wrong he was arrested one fine morning.

Franz Kafka, *The Trial*, 1925
Trans. by Willa and Edwin Muir, 1935

I first met him in Piraeus.

Nikos Kazantzakis, *Zorba the Greek*, 1946
Trans. by Carl Wildman, 1952

This is a book about the most admirable of human virtues—courage.

John F. Kennedy, *Profiles in Courage*, 1956

Riding up the winding road of Saint Agnes Cemetery in the back of the rattling old truck, Francis Phelan became aware that the dead, even more than the living, settled down in neighborhoods.

William Kennedy, *Ironweed,* **1983**

I first met Dean not long after my wife and I split up.

Jack Kerouac, *On the Road,* **1957**

The power to become habituated to his surroundings is a marked characteristic of mankind.

John Maynard Keynes, *The Economic Consequences of the Peace,* **1920**

Once upon a time, not so long ago, a monster came to the small town of Castle Rock, Maine.

Stephen King, *Cujo,* **1981**

I went back to Devon School not long ago, and found it looking oddly newer than when I was a student there fifteen years before.

John Knowles, *A Separate Peace,* **1959**

The cell door slammed behind Rubashov.

Arthur Koestler, *Darkness at Noon*, 1941
Trans. by Daphne Hardy, 1941

My name is Karim Amir, and I am an Englishman born and bred, almost.

Hanif Kureishi, *The Buddha of Suburbia*, 1990

Friend Al: Well, Al old pal I suppose you seen in the paper where I been sold to the White Sox.

Ring Lardner, "You Know Me Al," 1914

Ours is essentially a tragic age, so we refuse to take it tragically.

D. H. Lawrence, *Lady Chatterley's Lover,* 1928

Some of the evil of my tale may have been inherent in our circumstances.

T. E. Lawrence, *Seven Pillars of Wisdom,* 1926

Afterwards, in the dusty little corners where London's secret servants drink together, there was argument about where the Dolphin case history should really begin.

John le Carré, *The Honourable Schoolboy,* 1977

It was the evening on which MM. Debienne and Poligny, the managers of the Opera, were giving a last gala performance to mark their retirement.

Gaston Leroux, *The Phantom of the Opera*, 1910
Translator unknown

The two women were alone in the London flat.

Doris Lessing, *Free Women*, in *The Golden Notebook*, 1962

No, no, I can't tell you everything.

Primo Levi, *The Monkey's Wrench*, 1978
Trans. by William Weaver, 1986

On a hill by the Mississippi where Chippewas camped two generations ago, a girl stood in relief against the cornflower blue of Northern sky.

Sinclair Lewis, chapter 1, *Main Street*, 1920

The towers of Zenith aspired above the morning mist; austere towers of steel and cement and limestone, sturdy as cliffs and delicate as silver rods.

Sinclair Lewis, *Babbitt*, 1922

Four score and seven years ago our fathers brought forth on this continent, a new nation, conceived in Liberty, and dedicated to the proposition that all men are created equal.

Abraham Lincoln, Gettysburg Address, 1863

Night already shadows the eastern sky.

Charles A. Lindbergh, *The Spirit of St. Louis*, 1953

Buck did not read the newspapers, or he would have known that trouble was brewing, not alone for himself, but for every tidewater dog, strong of muscle and with warm, long hair, from Puget Sound to San Diego.

Jack London, *The Call of the Wild*, 1903

Two mountain chains traverse the republic roughly from north to south, forming between them a number of valleys and plateaus.

Malcolm Lowry, *Under the Volcano*, 1947

On a cold blowy February day a woman is boarding the ten A.M. flight to London, followed by an invisible dog.

Alison Lurie, *Foreign Affairs*, 1984

It was June, 1933, one week after Commencement, when Kay Leiland Strong, Vassar '33, the first of her class to run around the table at the Class Day dinner, was married to Harald Petersen, Reed '27, in the chapel of St. George's Church, P.E., Karl F. Reiland, Rector.

Mary McCarthy, *The Group*, 1963

In the town there were two mutes, and they were always together.

Carson McCullers, *The Heart Is a Lonely Hunter*, 1940

They, that desire to ingratiate themselves with a Prince, commonly use to offer themselves to his view, with things of that nature, as such persons take most pleasure and delight in: whereupon wee see they are many times presented with Horses and Armes, cloth of gold, pretious stones, and such like ornaments worthy of their greatnesse.

Niccolò Machiavelli, *The Prince*, 1513
Trans. by Edward Dacres, 1640

You are not the kind of guy who would be at a place like this at this time of the morning.

Jay McInerney, *Bright Lights, Big City,* **1984**

Nobody could sleep.

Norman Mailer, *The Naked and the Dead,* **1948**

Roy Hobbs pawed at the glass before thinking to prick a match with his thumbnail and hold the spurting flame in his cupped palm close to the lower berth window, but by then he had figured it was a tunnel they were passing through and was no longer surprised at the bright sight of himself holding a yellow light over his head, peering back in.

Bernard Malamud, *The Natural,* **1952**

From the small crossed window of his room above the table in the brickyard, Yakov Bok saw people in their own overcoats running somewhere early that morning, everybody in the same direction.

Bernard Malamud, *The Fixer,* **1966**

It befell in the days of Uther Pendragon, when he was king of all England, and so reigned, that there was a mighty duke in Cornwall that held war against him long time.

Sir Thomas Malory, *Le Morte d'Arthur,* **1485**

Diederich Hessling was a dreamy, delicate child, frightened of everything, and troubled frequently by earache.

Heinrich Mann, *Man of Straw,* **1918**
Trans. by Ernst Boyd, 1946

"And—and—what comes next?"

Thomas Mann, *Buddenbrooks,* **1901**
Trans. by H. T. Lowe-Porter, 1924

On a spring afternoon in 19—, the year in which for months on end so grave a threat seemed to hang over the peace of Europe, Gustave Aschenbach, or von Aschenbach as he had been officially known since his fiftieth birthday, had set out from his apartment on the Prinzregentenstrasse in Munich to take a walk of some length by himself.

Thomas Mann, *Death in Venice,* **1911**
Trans. by David Luke, 1988

An unassuming young man was travelling, in midsummer, from his native city of Hamburg to Davos-Platz in the Canton of Grisons, on a three weeks' visit.

Thomas Mann, *The Magic Mountain*, 1924
Trans. by H. T. Lowe-Porter, 1927

And after all the weather was ideal.

Katherine Mansfield, "The Garden Party," 1922

Charles Gray had not thought for a long time, consciously at least, about Clyde, Massachusetts, and he sometimes wondered later what caused him to do so one morning in mid-April, 1947.

John P. Marquand, *Point of No Return*, 1949

Dobbs Ferry possesses a rat which slips out of his lair at night and runs a typewriting machine in a garage.

Don Marquis, *archy and mehitabel*, 1927

In the somnolent July afternoon the unbroken line of brownstone houses down the long Brooklyn street resembled an army massed at attention.

Paule Marshall, *Brown Girl, Brownstones,* **1961**

A spectre is haunting Europe—the spectre of Communism.

Karl Marx and Friedrich Engels, *The Communist Manifesto,* **1848**
Trans. by Samuel Moore, 1888

Hegel remarks somewhere that all great, world-historical facts and personnages occur, as it were, twice. He has forgotten to add: the first time as tragedy, the second as farce.

Karl Marx, *The Eighteenth Brumaire of Louis Bonaparte,* **1852**
Translator unknown

From the Baltic city of St. Petersburg, built on a river marsh in a far northern corner of the empire, the Tsar ruled Russia.

Robert K. Massie, *Nicholas and Alexandra,* **1967**

The day broke grey and dull.

W. Somerset Maugham, *Of Human Bondage,* **1915**

I have never begun a novel with more misgiving.

W. Somerset Maugham, *The Razor's Edge,* **1944**

People called him Saint-Antoine—St. Anthony—partly because Antoine happened to be his name, partly because he was a jolly companion, a stout trencherman, and a hearty drinker, with a turn for practical joking and an eye for a petticoat, and this despite the fact that he was over sixty.

Guy de Maupassant, "Saint Anthony," 1873
Trans. by Marjorie Laurie, 1923

I sit in a pitch-pine panelled kitchen-living room, with an otter asleep upon its back among the cushions on the sofa, forepaws in the air, and with the expression of tightly shut concentration that very small babies wear in sleep.

Gavin Maxwell, *Ring of Bright Water,* **1961**

Call me Ishmael.

Herman Melville, *Moby-Dick,* **1851**

Alfieri: You wouldn't have known it, but something amusing has just happened.

Arthur Miller, *A View From the Bridge,* **1955**

Here is Edward Bear, coming downstairs now, bump, bump, bump, on the back of his head, behind Christopher Robin.

A. A. Milne, *Winnie-the-Pooh,* **1926**

> Of Mans First Disobedience, and the Fruit
> Of that Forbidden Tree, whose mortal tast
> Brought Death into the World, and all our woe,
> With loss of *Eden,* till one greater Man
> Restore us, and regain the blissful Seat,
> Sing Heav'nly Muse, that on the secret top
> Of *Oreb,* or of *Sinai,* didst inspire
> That Shepherd, who first taught the chosen Seed,
> In the beginning how the Heav'ns and Earth
> Rose out of *Chaos:* or if *Sion* Hill
> Delight thee more, and *Siloa's* Brook that flow'd

Fast by the Oracle of God; I thence
Invoke thy aid to my adventrous Song,
That with no middle flight intends to soar
Above th' *Aonian* Mount, while it pursue
Things unattempted yet in Prose or Rhime.

John Milton, *Paradise Lost*, CA. 1667

It was the rainy season in Bangkok.

Yukio Mishima, *The Temple of Dawn*, 1970
Trans. by E. Dale Saunders and Cecilia Segawa Seigle, 1973

Scarlett O'Hara was not beautiful, but men seldom realized it when caught by her charm as the Tarleton twins were.

Margaret Mitchell, *Gone With the Wind*, 1936

Death, they say, acquits us of all our obligations.

Michel de Montaigne, "That Intention Is Judge of Our Actions,"
***The Complete Essays of Montaigne*, 1580**
Trans. by Donald M. Frame, 1958

In a certain reign there was a lady not of the first rank whom the emperor loved more than any of the others.

Murasaki Shikibu, ***The Tale of Genji,*** **CA. 11TH CENTURY**
Trans. by Edward G. Seidensticker, 1976

"You're sure she doesn't know?" said George.

Iris Murdock, ***A Severed Head,*** **1961**

There was a depression over the Atlantic.

Robert Musil, ***The Man Without Qualities,*** **1930**
Trans. by Eithne Wilkins and Ernst Kaiser, 1953–60

N

Lolita, light of my life, fire of my loins.

Vladimir Nabokov, *Lolita,* **1955**

As soon as our quarantine flag came down and the last of the barefooted, blue-uniformed policemen of the Bombay Port Health Authority had left the ship, Coelho the Goan came aboard and, luring me with a long beckoning finger into the saloon, whispered, "You have any cheej?"

V. S. Naipaul, *An Area of Darkness,* **1964**

The world is what it is; men who are nothing, who allow themselves to become nothing, have no place in it.

V. S. Naipaul, *A Bend in the River,* **1979**

When Zarathustra was thirty years old, he left his home and the lake of his home and went into the mountains.

Friedrich Nietzsche, *Thus Spake Zarathustra,* **1885**
Trans. by R. J. Hollingdale, 1961

The British are frequently criticized by other nations for their dislike of change, and indeed we love England for those aspects of nature and life which change the least.

Charles Nordhoff and James Norman Hall, *Mutiny on the Bounty,* **1932**

The grandmother didn't want to go to Florida.

Flannery O'Connor, "A Good Man Is Hard to Find," 1955

The cocks had just heralded the break of day when the first clap of thunder burst above Black Valley.

Liam O'Flaherty, *Famine*, 1937

Our story opens in the mind of Luther L. (for Le Roy) Fleigler, who is lying in his bed, not thinking of anything, but just aware of sounds, conscious of his own breathing, and sensitive to his own heartbeat.

John O'Hara, *Appointment in Samarra*, 1934

Wake!

Omar Khayyám, *Rubáiyát*, 11TH CENTURY
Trans. by Edward Fitzgerald, 1859

Tyrone: You're a fine armful now, Mary, with those twenty pounds you've gained.

Eugene O'Neill, *Long Day's Journey Into Night,* **1956**

Mr Jones, of the Manor Farm, had locked the hen-houses for the night, but was too drunk to remember to shut the pop-holes.

George Orwell, *Animal Farm,* **1945**

It was a bright cold day in April, and the clocks were striking thirteen.

George Orwell, *1984,* **1949**

These are the times that try men's souls: The summer soldier and the sunshine patriot will, in this crisis, shrink from the service of their country; but he that stands it NOW, deserves the thanks of man and woman.

Thomas Paine, *American Crisis,* **1776**

On they went, singing "Rest Eternal," and whenever they stopped, their feet, the horses, and the gusts of wind seemed to carry on their singing.

Boris Pasternak, *Doctor Zhivago,* **1957**
Trans. by Manya Harari and Max Hayward, 1958

There is a lovely road that runs from Ixopo into the hills.

Alan Paton, *Cry, the Beloved Country,* **1948**

Perhaps I could have saved him, with only a word, two words, out of my mouth.

Alan Paton, *Too Late the Phalarope,* **1953**

All of us, at some moment, have had a vision of our existence as something unique, untransferable, and very precious.

Octavio Paz, *The Labyrinth of Solitude,* **1950**
Trans. by Lysander Kemp, 1961

This morning (we lying lately in the garret) I rose, put on my suit with great skirts, having not lately worn any other clothes but them.

Samuel Pepys, *The Diary of Samuel Pepys,* POSTHUMOUS, **1825 [1660]**
Edited and transcribed by Robert Latham and William Matthews, 1970

It was a queer, sultry summer, the summer they electrocuted the Rosenbergs, and I didn't know what I was doing in New York.

Sylvia Plath, *The Bell Jar,* **1963**

Socrates: To what degree, Gentlemen of Athens, you have been affected by my accusers, I do not know. I, at any rate, was almost led to forget who I am—so convincingly did they speak. Yet hardly anything they have said is true.

Plato, "The Speech of Defense" (17a–35d), CA. 399 B.C.
Trans. by R. E. Allen, 1984

A s geographers, Sosius, crowd into the edges of their maps parts of the world which they do not know about, adding notes in the margin to the effect, that beyond this lies nothing but the sandy deserts full of wild beasts, unapproachable bogs, Sythian ice, or a frozen sea, so in this work of mine, in which I have compared the lives of the greatest men with one another, after passing through those periods which probable reasoning can reach to and real history find a footing in, I might very well say of those that are farther off: Beyond this there is nothing but prodigies and fictions, the only inhabitants are the poets and inventors of fables; there is no credit, or certainty any farther.

Plutarch, "Theseus," *Plutarch's Lives* [*The Lives of the Noble Greeks and Romans*], 1579
Trans. by John Dryden, rev. by Hugh Clough, 1864

It should be known to the general reader that, at the time when Baldwin II. was emperor of Constantinople, where a magistrate representing the doge of Venice then resided, and in the year of our Lord 1260, Nicolo Polo, the father of the said Marco, and Maffeo, the brother of Nicolo, respectable and well-informed men, embarked on a ship of their own, with a rich and varied cargo of merchandise, and reached Constantinople in safety.

Marco Polo, *The Travels of Marco Polo,* ca. 1299
Edited by Manuel Komroff, after W. Marsden translation, 1926

She was a spirited-looking young woman, with dark curly hair cropped and parted on the side, a short oval face with straight eyebrows, and a large curved mouth.

Katherine Anne Porter, "Old Mortality," *Pale Horse, Pale Rider,* **1939**

People do not give it credence that a fourteen-year-old girl could leave her home and go off in the wintertime to avenge her father's blood but it did not seem so strange then, although I will say it did not happen every day.

Charles Portis, *True Grit,* **1968**

To explain how my Uncle Nick asked me to join him, I have to go back to my mother's funeral.

J. B. Priestly, *Lost Empires,* **1965**

For a long time I used to go to bed early.

Marcel Proust, *Swann's Way, Remembrance of Things Past,* **1913–27**
Trans. by C. K. Scott Moncrieff, rev. by Terence Kilmartin, 1981

—Something a little strange, that's what you notice, that she's not a woman like all the others.

Manuel Puig, *Kiss of the Spider Woman,* **1976**
Trans. by Thomas Colchie, 1979

Amerigo Bonasera sat in New York Criminal Court Number 3 and waited for justice; vengeance on the men who had so cruelly hurt his daughter, who had tried to dishonor her.

Mario Puzo, *The Godfather,* **1969**

A screaming comes across the sky.

Thomas Pynchon, *Gravity's Rainbow,* **1973**

I send you back to the Great Pantagrueline Chronicle, if you would form an idea of the genealogy of Gargantua and of the antiquity from which he has come down to us.

François Rabelais, *Gargantua*, book 2, 1532–64
Trans. by Thomas Urquhart, 1653

We are at rest five miles behind the front.

Erich Maria Remarque, *All Quiet on the Western Front*, 1928
Trans. by A. W. Wheen, 1929

The Citadel of Troizen, where the Palace stands, was built by giants before anyone remembers.

Mary Renault, *The King Must Die*, 1958

Bright, clear sky over a plain so wide that the rim of the heavens cut down on it around the entire horizon. . . .

O. E. Rölvaag, *Giants in the Earth,* **1924–25**
Trans. by Lincoln Colcord and the author, 1927

She was so deeply imbedded in my consciousness that for the first year of school I seem to have believed that each of my teachers was my mother in disguise.

Philip Roth, *Portnoy's Complaint,* **1969**

I mean to inquire if, in the civil order, there can be any sure and legitimate rule of administration, men being taken as they are and laws as they may be.

Jean Jacques Rousseau, *The Social Contract,* **1762**
Trans. by G. D. H. Cole, 1913

Man is born free; and everywhere he is in chains.

Jean Jacques Rousseau, chapter 1, *The Social Contract,* **1762**
Trans. by G. D. H. Cole, 1913

One evening along toward seven o'clock, many citizens are standing out on Broadway in front of Mindy's restaurant, speaking of one thing and another, and particularly about the tough luck they have playing the races in the afternoon, when who comes up the street with a little doll hanging onto his right thumb but a guy by the name of Sorrowful.

Damon Runyon, "Little Miss Marker," 1934

"To be born again," sang Gibreel Farishta tumbling from the heavens, "first you have to die."

Salman Rushdie, *The Satanic Verses*, 1988

Is there any knowledge in the world which is so certain that no reasonable man could doubt it?

Bertrand Russell, *The Problems of Philosophy*, 1912

He was born with the gift of laughter and the sense that the world was mad, and that was his only patrimony.

Rafael Sabatini, *Scaramouche,* **1921**

There were two sisters very unlike each other.

Marquis de Sade, *Justine,* **1791**
Trans. by Richard Seaver and Austryn Wainhouse, 1965

The world is very old, and human beings are very young.

Carl Sagan, *The Dragons of Eden,* **1977**

We had spent the afternoon in a café on the Rue Saint-Jacques, a spring afternoon just like any other.

Françoise Sagan, *A Certain Smile,* **1956**
Trans. by Anne Green, 1956

Francesca Bassington sat in the drawing-room of her house in Blue Street, W., regaling herself and her estimable brother Henry with China tea and small cress sandwiches.

Saki, *The Unbearable Bassington,* **1912**

If you really want to hear about it, the first thing you'll probably want to know is where I was born, and what my lousy childhood was like, and how my parents were occupied and all before they had me, and all that David Copperfield kind of crap, but I don't feel like going into it, if you want to know the truth.

J. D. Salinger, *The Catcher in the Rye,* **1951**

In the year 1776, when the thirteen American colonies gave to the world that famous piece of paper known as the Declaration of Independence, there was a captain of Virginia militia living in Rockingham County, named Abraham Lincoln.

Carl Sandburg, *Abraham Lincoln: The Prairie Years,* **1926**

The famous lawyer, Rufus Choate, listening to foreign-language grand opera in New York, had just told his daughter to be sure to let him know when to laugh or cry or just sit still and keep cool.

Carl Sandburg, *Abraham Lincoln: The War Years,* **1939**

A little below the State House in Boston, where Beacon Street consents to bend slightly and begins to run down hill, and where across the Mall the grassy shoulder of the Common slopes most steeply down to the Frog Pond, there stood about the year 1870—and for all I know there may still stand—a pair of old brick houses, flatter and plainer than the rest.

George Santayana, *The Last Puritan, A Memoir in the Form of a Novel*, 1935

The little boy named Ulysses Macauley one day stood over the new gopher hole in the backyard of his house on Santa Clara Avenue in Ithaca, California.

William Saroyan, *The Human Comedy*, 1943

Our inquiry has led us to the heart of being.

Jean-Paul Sartre, *Being and Nothingness*, 1943
Trans. by Hazel E. Barnes, 1956

I have said that Spring arrived late in 1916, and that up in the trenches opposite Mametz it seemed as though Winter would last for ever.

Siegfried Sassoon, *Memoirs of an Infantry Officer*, 1930

Lord Peter Wimsey stretched himself luxuriously between the sheets provided by the Hôtel Meurice.

Dorothy L. Sayers, *Clouds of Witness*, 1926

The first time I saw him he couldn't have been much more than sixteen years old, a little ferret of a kid, sharp and quick.

Budd Schulberg, *What Makes Sammy Run?* 1941

Our eyes register the light of dead stars.

André Schwarz-Bart, *The Last of the Just*, 1959
Trans. by Stephen Becker, 1960

In that pleasant district of merry England which is watered by the river Don, there extended in ancient times a large forest, covering the greater part of the beautiful hills and valleys which lie between Sheffield and the pleasant town of Doncaster.

Sir Walter Scott, *Ivanhoe*, 1819

What can you say about a twenty-four-year-old girl who died?

Erich Segal, *Love Story*, 1970

Ilka had been three months in this country when she went West and discovered her first American sitting on a stool in a bar in the desert, across from the railroad.

Lore Segal, *Her First American,* **1985**

Gloucester:
Now is the winter of our discontent
Made glorious summer by this sun of York;
And all the clouds that loured upon our house
In the deep bosom of the ocean buried.

William Shakespeare, *King Richard the Third,* CA. **1592**

Flavius:
Hence! home, you idle creatures, get you home!

William Shakespeare, *Julius Caesar,* **1599**

Duke:
If music be the food of love, play on;
Give me excess of it, that, surfeiting,
The appetite may sicken, and so die.

William Shakespeare, *Twelfth Night,* CA. **1602**

First witch:
When shall we three meet again?
In thunder, lightning, or in rain?

William Shakespeare, *Macbeth,* **CA. 1606**

Robert: No eggs! No eggs!! Thousand thunders, man, what do you mean by no eggs?

George Bernard Shaw, *Saint Joan,* **1924**

You will rejoice to hear that no disaster has accompanied the commencement of an enterprise which you have regarded with such evil forebodings.

Mary Shelley, *Frankenstein; or, The Modern Prometheus,* **1818**

On the very eve of the birth of the Third Reich a feverish tension gripped Berlin.

William L. Shirer, *The Rise and Fall of the Third Reich,* **1960**

The Melekhov farm was right at the end of Tatarsk village.

Mikhail Sholokhov, *And Quiet Flows the Don,* **1928**
Trans. by Stephen Garry, 1962

Petronius woke only about midday, and as usual greatly wearied.

Henryk Sienkiewicz, *Quo Vadis,* **1895**
Trans. by Jeremiah Curtin, 1896

Herman Broder turned over and opened one eye.

Isaac Bashevis Singer, *Enemies, A True Story,* **1972**

Serene was a word you could put to Brooklyn, New York.

Betty Smith, *A Tree Grows in Brooklyn,* **1943**

In a certain county of England, bounded on one side by the sea, and at the distance of one hundred miles from the metropolis, lived Gamaliel Pickle Esq; the father of that hero whose adventures we propose to record.

Tobias Smollett, *The Adventures of Peregrine Pickle,* **1751**

That afternoon I had been walking with my son in what for me were familiar streets, streets of the town where I was born.

C. P. Snow, *The Sleep of Reason,* **1968**

Reveille was sounded, as always, at 5 A.M.—a hammer pounding on a rail outside camp HQ.

Aleksandr I. Solzhenitsyn, *One Day in the Life of Ivan Denisovitch*, 1962
Trans. by Max Hayward and Ronald Hingley, 1963

On top of everything, the cancer wing was Number 13.

Aleksandr I. Solzhenitsyn, *Cancer Ward*, 1968
Trans. by Nicholas Bethell and David Burg, 1968

> Son of Agamemnon, once general at Troy,
> now you are here, now you can see it all,
> all that your heart has always longed for.
>
> **Sophocles, *Electra*, CA. 414 B.C.**
> *Trans. by David Grene, 1959*

The boys, as they talked to the girls from Marcia Blaine School, stood on the far side of their bicycles holding the handlebars, which established a protective fence of bicycle between the sexes, and the impression that at any moment the boys were likely to be away.

Muriel Spark, *The Prime of Miss Jean Brodie*, 1961

Soon you're going to have a baby.

Dr. Benjamin Spock, *Dr. Spock's Baby and Child Care,* **1945**

To the red country and part of the gray country of Oklahoma, the last rains came gently, and they did not cut the scarred earth.

John Steinbeck, *The Grapes of Wrath,* **1939**

Cannery Row in Monterey in California is a poem, a stink, a grating noise, a quality of light, a tone, a habit, a nostalgia, a dream.

John Steinbeck, *Cannery Row,* **1945**

On the 15th of May, 1796, General Bonaparte made his entry into Milan at the head of that young army which had shortly before crossed the Bridge of Lodi and taught the world that after all these centuries Caesar and Alexander had a successor.

Stendhal, *The Charterhouse of Palma,* **1839**
Trans. by C. K. Scott Moncrieff, 1924

I wish either my father or my mother, or indeed both of them, as they were in duty both equally bound to it, had minded what they were about when they begot me; had they duly considered how much depended upon what they were then doing;—that not only the production of a rational Being was concerned in it, but that possibly the happy formation and temperature of his body, perhaps his genius and the very cast of his mind;—and, for aught they knew to the contrary, even the fortunes of his whole house might take their turn from the humours and dispositions which were then uppermost:— Had they duly weighted and considered all this, and proceeded accordingly,—I an verily persuaded I should have made a quite different figure in the world, from that, in which the reader is likely to see me.

Lawrence Sterne, *The Life and Opinions of Tristan Shandy, Gentleman*, 1759–67

I will begin the story of my adventures with a certain morning early in the month of June, the year of grace 1751, when I took the key for the last time out of the door of my father's house.

Robert Louis Stevenson, *Kidnapped*, 1886

Mr. Utterson the lawyer was a man of a rugged countenance that was never lighted by a smile; cold, scanty and embarrassed; in discourse; backward in sentiment; lean, long, dusty, dreary and yet somehow loveable.

Robert Louis Stevenson, *The Strange Case of Dr. Jekyll and Mr. Hyde*, 1886

Once, from eastern ocean to western ocean, the land stretched away without names.

George R. Stewart, *Names on the Land,* **1945**

"Monsieur Van Gogh! It's time to wake up!"

Irving Stone, *Lust for Life,* **1934**

There was only one bench in the shade and Converse went for it, although it was already occupied.

Robert Stone, *Dog Soldiers,* **1974**

The science of Geography, which I now propose to investigate, is, I think, quite as much as any other science, a concern to the philosopher; and the correctness of my view is clear for many reasons.

Strabo, *The Geography,* CA. 44 B.C.
Trans. by Horace Leonard Jones, 1917

In those days cheap apartments were almost impossible to find in Manhattan, so I had to move to Brooklyn.

William Styron, *Sophie's Choice,* **1979**

Warfare is the greatest affair of the state, the basis of life and death, the way [Tao] to survival or extinction. It must be thoroughly pondered and analyzed.

Sun-tzu, *The Art of War,* CA. **100** B.C.
Trans. by Ralph D. Sawyer, with Mei-chü Sawyer, 1993

My father had a small Estate in *Nottinghamshire;* I was the Third of five Sons.

Jonathan Swift, *Gulliver's Travels,* **1726**

It is a melancholy Object to those, who walk through this great Town, or travel in the Country; when they see the *Streets,* the *Roads,* and *Cabin-doors* crowded with *Beggars* of the Female Sex, followed by three, four, or six children, *all in Rags,* and importuning every Passenger for an Alms.

Jonathan Swift, "A Modest Proposal for Preventing the children of poor People in *Ireland,* from being a burden to their Parents or Country; and for making them beneficial to the Publick," 1729

T

In Rome's earliest years as a city, its rulers were kings.

Tacitus, *The Annals of Imperial Rome*, CA. 116
Trans. by Michael Grant, 1956

Major Amberson had "made a fortune" in 1873, when other people were losing fortunes, and the magnificence of the Ambersons began then.

Booth Tarkington, *The Magnificent Ambersons*, 1918

Leodogran, the king of Cameliard,
Had one fair daughter, and none other child;
And she was fairest of all flesh on earth,
Guinevere, and in her his one delight.

Alfred, Lord Tennyson, *Idylls of the King*, 1859–85

While the present century was in its teens, and on one sunshiny morning in June, there drove up to the great iron gate of Miss Pinkerton's academy for young ladies, on Chiswick Mall, a large family coach, with two fat horses in blazing harness, driven by a fat coachman in a three-cornered hat and wig, at the rate of four miles an hour.

William Makepeace Thackeray, *Vanity Fair,* **1848**

Ever since childhood, when I lived within earshot of the Boston and Maine, I have seldom heard a train go by and not wished I was on it.

Paul Theroux, *The Great Railway Bazaar,* **1975**

The grass-green cart, with "J. Jones, Gorsehill" painted shakily on it, stopped in the cobblestone passage between "The Hare's Foot" and "The Pure Drop."

Dylan Thomas, *Portrait of the Artist as a Young Dog,* **1940**

We were somewhere around Barstow on the edge of the desert when the drugs began to take hold.

Hunter S. Thompson, *Fear and Loathing in Las Vegas: A Savage Journey to the Heart of the American Dream,* **1971**

When I wrote the following pages, or rather the bulk of them, I lived alone, in the woods, a mile from any neighbour, in a house which I had built myself, on the shore of Walden Pond, in Concord, Massachusetts, and earned my living by the labour of my hands only.

Henry David Thoreau, *Walden,* **1854**

Once upon a Sunday there was a city mouse who went to visit a country mouse.

James Thurber, *Fables for Our Time,* **1940**

Amongst the novel objects that attracted my attention during my stay in the United States, nothing struck me more forcibly than the general equality of condition among the people.

Alexis de Tocqueville, *Democracy in America,* **1835–39**
Trans. by Henry Reeve, revised by Frances Bowen, n.d.

When Mr. Bilbo Baggins of Bag End announced that he would shortly be celebrating his eleventy-first birthday with a party of special magnificence, there was much talk and excitement in Hobbiton.

J. R. R. Tolkien, *The Fellowship of the Ring,* **1954**

"*Eh bien, mon prince,* so Genoa and Lucca are now no more than family estates of the Bonapartes."

Leo Tolstoy, *War and Peace,* **1864–69**
Trans. by Ann Dunnigan, 1968

Happy families are all alike; every unhappy family is unhappy in its own way.

Leo Tolstoy, *Anna Karenina,* **1873–76**
Trans. by Constance Garnett

When God began to create heaven and earth—the earth being unformed and void, with darkness over the surface of the deep and a wind from God sweeping over the water—God said, "Let there be light"; and there was light.

Torah, Genesis, from *Tanakh: A New Translation of the Holy Scriptures,* **1985**

The bench on which Dobbs was sitting was not so good.

B. Traven, *The Treasure of the Sierra Madre,* **1927**
Trans. by author, 1937

It is not easy to introduce myself.

William Trevor, *My House in Umbria,* **1991**

A woman, not yet fifty-seven and seeming frail, eats carefully at a table in a corner.

William Trevor, *Reading Turgenev,* **1991**

In the latter days of July in the year 185–, a most important question was for ten days hourly asked in the cathedral city of Barchester, and answered every hour in various ways—Who was to be the new bishop?

Anthony Trollope, *Barchester Towers,* **1857**

Childhood is looked upon as the happiest time of life.

Leon Trotsky, *My Life,* **1930**
Anonymous translator

So gorgeous was the spectacle on the May morning of 1910 when nine kings rode in the funeral of Edward VII of England that the crowd, waiting in hushed and black-clad awe, could not keep back gasps of admiration.

Barbara W. Tuchman, *The Guns of August,* **1962**

"Well, Peter, not in sight yet?" was the question asked on May 20th, 1859, by a gentleman a little over forty, in a dusty coat and checked trousers, who came out hatless to the low porch of the posting station at S———.

Ivan Turgenev, *Fathers and Sons,* **1862**
Trans. by Constance Garnett, revised by Ralph E. Matlaw, 1972

You don't know about me without you have read a book by the name of *The Adventures of Tom Sawyer,* but that ain't no matter.

Mark Twain, *The Adventures of Huckleberry Finn,* **1884**

Boys are playing basketball around a telephone pole with a backboard bolted to it.

John Updike, *Rabbit, Run,* **1960**

1. Valmiki, the ascetic, questioned the eloquent Narada, bull among sages, always devoted to asceticism and study of the sacred texts.

Vālmīki, "The Bālakānda," *The Rāmāyaṇa,* **CA. 500 B.C.**
Trans. by Robert P. Goldman, 1984

The institution of a leisure class is found in its best development at the higher stages of the barbarian culture; as, for instance, in feudal Europe or feudal Japan.

Thorstein Veblen, *The Theory of the Leisure Class,* **1899**

The year 1866 was marked by a strange event, an unexplainable occurrence which is undoubtedly still fresh in everyone's memory.

Jules Verne, *Twenty Thousand Leagues Under the Sea,* **1870**
Trans. by Anthony Bonner, 1962

I am Myra Breckinridge whom no man will ever possess.

Gore Vidal, *Myra Breckinridge,* **1968**

Arms and the man I sing, the first who came,
Compelled by fate, an exile out of Troy,
To Italy and the Lavinian coast,
Much buffeted on land and on the deep
By violence of the gods, through that long rage,
That lasting hate of Juno's.

Virgil, *The Aeneid*, 19 B.C.
Trans. by Rolfe Humphries, 1951

There lived in Westphalia, in the castle of the Baron of Thunder-ten-tronckh, a young man on whom nature had bestowed the perfection of perfect manners.

Voltaire, *Candide*, 1759
Trans. by Robert M. Adams, 1966

Call me Jonah.

Kurt Vonnegut, *Cat's Cradle*, 1963

To the as-yet-unborn, to all innocent wisps of undifferentiated nothing: Watch out for life.

Kurt Vonnegut, *Deadeye Dick*, 1982

You better not never tell nobody but God.

Alice Walker, *The Color Purple,* **1982**

The Jebel es Zubleh is a mountain fifty miles and more in length, and so narrow that its tracery on the map gives it a likeness to a caterpillar crawling from the south to the north.

Lew Wallace, *Ben-Hur,* **1880**

At the sight of her son Judith's eyes and mouth broke into the loveliest smile that any member of the Herries family, there present, had ever seen.

Hugh Walpole, *Vanessa,* **1933**

Sir, I have made so ill use of your former favours, as by them to be encouraged to entreat that they may be enlarged to the patronage and protection of this Book: and I have put on a modest confidence,

that I shall not be denied, because it is a discourse of Fish and
Fishing, which you know so well, and both love and practice so much.

Izaak Walton, *The Compleat Angler,* **1653**

Mason City.
To get there you follow Highway 58, going northeast out of the city,
and it is a good highway and new.

Robert Penn Warren, *All the King's Men,* **1946**

It was clearly going to be a bad crossing.

Evelyn Waugh, *Vile Bodies,* **1930**

"Was anyone hurt?"

Evelyn Waugh, *A Handful of Dust,* **1934**

No one would have believed in the last years of the nineteenth
century that this world was being watched keenly and closely by
intelligences greater than man's and yet as mortal as our own; that as
men busied themselves about their various concerns they were
scrutinised and studied, perhaps almost as narrowly as a man with a

microscope might scrutinise the transient creatures that swarm and multiply in a drop of water.

H. G. Wells, *The War of the Worlds,* **1898**

The nickname of the train was the Yellow Dog.

Eudora Welty, *Delta Wedding,* **1946**

It was his profession to prepare other men for death; it shocked him to be so unready for his own.

Morris West, *The Devil's Advocate,* **1959**

I had the story, bit by bit, from various people, and, as generally happens in such cases, each time it was a different story.

Edith Wharton, *Ethan Frome,* **1911**

On a January evening of the early seventies, Christine Nilsson was singing in Faust at the Academy of Music in New York.

Edith Wharton, *The Age of Innocence,* **1920**

"Where's Papa going with that ax?" said Fern to her mother as they were setting the table for breakfast.

E. B. White, *Charlotte's Web*, 1952

I celebrate myself
And what I assume you shall assume,
For every atom belonging to me as good belongs to you.

Walt Whitman, "Song of Myself," 1855

On Friday noon, July the twentieth, 1714, the finest bridge in all Peru broke and precipitated five travellers into the gulf below.

Thornton Wilder, *The Bridge of San Luis Rey*, 1927

At five o'clock in the afternoon, which was late in March, the stainless blue of the sky over Rome had begun to pale and the blue transparency of the narrow streets had gathered a faint opacity of vapor.

Tennessee Williams, *The Roman Spring of Mrs. Stone*, 1950

Some notable sight was drawing the passengers, both men and women, to the window; and therefore I rose and crossed the car to see what it was.

Owen Wister, *The Virginian*, 1902

"Yes, of course, if it's fine tomorrow," said Mrs. Ramsey.
   Virginia Woolf, *To the Lighthouse,* **1927**

The sun had not yet risen.
   Virginia Woolf, *The Waves,* **1931**

Dere's no guy livin' dat knows Brooklyn t'roo an' t'roo, because it'd take a guy a lifetime just to find his way aroun' duh f—— town.
   Thomas Wolfe, "Only the Dead Know Brooklyn," 1932

It was the hour of twilight on a soft spring day toward the end of April in the year of Our Lord 1929, and George Webber leaned his elbows on the sill of his back window and looked out at what he could see of New York.
   Thomas Wolfe, *You Can't Go Home Again,* **1940**

He was of medium height, somewhat chubby, and good looking, with curly red hair and an innocent, gay face, more remarkable for a humorous air about the eyes and large mouth than for any strength of chin or nobility of nose.
   Herman Wouk, *The Caine Mutiny,* **1951**

Customs of courtship vary greatly in different times and places, but the way the thing happens to be done here and now seems the only natural way to do it.

Herman Wouk, *Marjorie Morningstar,* **1955**

Mr. George Lawrence, C.M.G., First Class District Officer of His Majesty's Civil Service, sat at the door of his tent and viewed the African desert scene with the eye of extreme disfavour.

Percival Christopher Wren, *Beau Geste,* **1924**

Brrrrrrriiiiiiiiiiiiiiiiinng!

Richard Wright, *Native Son,* **1940**

One winter morning in the long-ago, four-year-old days of my life I found myself standing before a fireplace, warming my hands over a mound of glowing coals, listening to the wind whistling past the house outside.

Richard Wright, *Black Boy,* **1945**

At nine o'clock the auditorium of the Théâtre des Variétés was still virtually empty; a few people were waiting in the dress circle and the stalls, lost among the red velvet armchairs, in the half-light of the dimly glowing chandelier.

Emile Zola, *Nana,* **1880**
Trans. by George Holden, 1972

LAST LINES

A

The guy we counted on, well, he moved on.
Edward Abbey, *Black Sun*, 1971

"And don't forget to cut the fucking deck."
Edward Abbey, *The Monkey Wrench Gang*, 1975

Perhaps some day—say 1938, their centenary—they might be allowed to return together for a holiday, to see the mistakes of their successors; and perhaps then, for the first time since man began his education among the carnivores, they would find a world that sensitive and timid natures could regard without a shudder.

Henry Adams, *The Education of Henry Adams*, 1918

Hazel followed; and together they slipped away, running easily down through the wood, where the first primroses were beginning to bloom.

Richard Adams, *Watership Down*, 1972

But he did not ask, and his uncle did not speak except to say, after a few minutes, "It's time to go home," and all the way home they walked in silence.

James Agee, *A Death in the Family*, 1957

Pausing an instant on the threshold before she vanished from their sight, she looked backward, and fixing on Gerald the strange glance he remembered well, she said in her penetrating voice, "Is not the last scene better than the first?"

Louisa May Alcott, "Behind a Mask; or, A Woman's Power," 1866

"Oh, my girls, however long you may live, I never can wish you a greater happiness than this!"

Louisa May Alcott, *Little Women*, 1868–69

(*A dream, they say, of a golden arm*
That belonged to the dealer we called Machine.)

Nelson Algren, *The Man With the Golden Arm*, 1949

In that hour that frogs begin and the scent off the mesquite comes strongest.

Nelson Algren, *A Walk on the Wild Side*, 1956

The train ran into a tunnel.

Eric Ambler, *A Coffin for Dimitrios*, 1939

I put on my dinner-jacket, swallowed a strong whisky, and went downstairs to begin the evening round.

Kingsley Amis, *The Green Man*, 1969

He stayed that way for a long time and when he aroused himself and again looked out of the car window the town of Winesburg had disappeared and his life there had become but a background on which to paint the dreams of his manhood.

Sherwood Anderson, "Departure," *Winesburg, Ohio*, 1919

When I look back for one last glimpse of Jesus, he is nearing the rafters, ascending still.

Max Apple, *Zip,* **1978**

Again, we do not know where these developments will lead us, but we know, or should know, that every decrease in power is an open invitation to violence—if only because those who hold power and feel it slipping from their hands, be they the government or be they the governed, have always found it difficult to resist the temptation to substitute violence for it.

Hannah Arendt, *On Violence,* **1970**

Released from its body, now ice-cold, the angry spirit which, among the living, had been so proud and insolent, fled cursing down to the dismal shores of Acheron.

Lodovico Ariosto, *Orlando Furioso,* **1532**
Trans. by Guido Waldman, 1974

It is clear, then, that we have these three goals to aim at in education—the happy mean, the possible, and the appropriate.

Aristotle, *The Politics,* **323 B.C.**
Trans. by Carnes Lord, 1984

It did make a mess; but then, I don't think I'll ever be a tidy person.
Margaret Atwood, *Lady Oracle,* **1976**

And I must shut with a man's firmness a journal which seems the safest of self-indulgences in contrast to the austerely empty notebook that now I open.

Louis Auchincloss, *The Rector of Justin,* **1964**

"Maama, Maaama, Maamaaa!"
Jean M. Auel, *The Clan of the Cave Bear,* **1980**

Let those who think I have said too little, or those who think I have said too much, forgive me; and let those who think I have said just enough join me in giving thanks to God. Amen.

Saint Augustine, *The City of God,* CA. **426**
Trans. by Marcus Dods, 1909

Darcy, as well as Elizabeth, really loved them; and they were both ever sensible of the warmest gratitude towards the persons who, by bringing her into Derbyshire, had been the means of uniting them.

Jane Austen, *Pride and Prejudice*, 1813

But, in spite of these deficiencies, the wishes, the hopes, the confidence, the predictions of the small band of true friends who witnessed the ceremony, were fully answered in the perfect happiness of the union.

Jane Austen, *Emma*, 1816

We walked up the stairs together, and once we were inside, I handed him the pages of this book.

Paul Auster, *Leviathan*, 1992

The day had barely begun.
Richard Bach, *One,* **1988**

Yet, as I turn and begin walking toward the waiting people, the wind blows some of them back to me.

James Baldwin, *Giovanni's Room,* **1956**

Then, as a first challenge to Society, Restignac went to dine with Mme. de Nucingen.

Honoré de Balzac, *Le Père Goriot,* **1834**
Trans. by Ellen Marriage, 1907

Pray excuse the faults of the copyist!
Honoré de Balzac, *Cousin Pons,* **1847**
Trans. by William Walton, 1896

Go, my book, and help destroy the world as it is.
   Russell Banks, *Continental Drift,* **1985**

Yes, I am happy that my sons will not be seamen. . . . and yet . . .
   Pió Baroja, *The Restlessness of Shanti Andía,* **1911**
   Trans. by Anthony and Elaine Kerrigan, 1959

"He was not of our faith, nor of our skin," she says, "but he was a man of greatness, of an utter devotion."
   William E. Barrett, *The Lilies of the Field,* **1962**

When Margaret grows up she will have a daughter, who is to be Peter's mother in turn; and thus it will go on, so long as children are gay and innocent and heartless.
   J. M. Barrie, *Peter Pan* [*Peter Pan and Wendy*], **1911**

Therefore he will construct funhouses for others and be their secret operator—though he would rather be among the lovers for whom funhouses are designed.
   John Barth, "Lost in the Funhouse," 1967

I am Grim Fiddle, and in a hurry, and very, very lucky for it.

John Calvin Batchelor, *The Birth of the People's Republic of Antarctica,* **1983**

"And oh, Aunt Em! I'm so glad to be at home again!"

L. Frank Baum, *The Wonderful Wizard of Oz,* **1900**

Clorin: And to thee
All thy master's love be free!

Francis Beaumont and John Fletcher,
The Faithful Shepherdess, **1609**

Who knows?

Simone de Beauvoir, *The Mandarins,* **1954**
Trans. by Leonard M. Friedman, 1956

Fortunate is he who, with a case so desperate as mine, finds a judge so merciful.

Edward Bellamy, *Looking Backward,* **1888**

I guess I felt it was my turn now to move, and so went running—leaping, leaping, pounding, and tingling over the pure white lining of the gray Arctic silence.

Saul Bellow, *Henderson the Rain King,* **1959**

Not a single word.

Saul Bellow, *Herzog,* **1964**

"They must be crocuses."

Saul Bellow, *Humboldt's Gift,* **1975**

She glanced at the soup-plate, and, on the chance that it might after all contain something worth inspection, she awkwardly balanced herself on her old legs and went to it again.

Arnold Bennett, *The Old Wives' Tale,* **1908**

Possibly all is for the best.

E. F. Benson, *The Freaks of Mayfair,* **1916**

Swa beʒnornodon   ʒeata leode
hlafordes [hry]re,   heorð-ʒeneatas;
ewædon þæ he wære   wyruld-cyninʒ,
manna mildust   ond mon-[ðw]ærust,
leodum liðost,   ond lof- ʒeornost.

Beowulf, ca. 800

Thus his fellow Geats,
Chosen champions   cheerlessly grieved
for the loss of their lord,   leader and defender.
They called him of captains,   kings of the known world,
of men most generous   and most gracious,
kindest to his clansmen   and questing for praise.

Trans. by Ruth M. Lehmann, 1988

The grace of Our Lord Jesus Christ be with you all. Amen.

The Bible, King James Version, 1611

Peyton Farquhar was dead; his body, with a broken neck, swung gently from side to side beneath the timbers of the Owl Creek bridge.

Ambrose Bierce, "An Occurrence at Owl Creek Bridge," 1891

Here ends the tenth and last day of the book called
                    Decameron, also known as *Prince Galeotto.*

Giovanni Boccaccio, *The Decameron,* 1353
Trans. by Mark Musa and Peter Bondanella, 1977

I put it back where it belonged and went on singing.

Heinrich Böll, *The Clown,* 1963
Trans. by Leila Vennewitz, 1965

Let me commit myself to the care of my merciful Creator.

James Boswell, *Boswell's London Journal, 1762–63,* POSTHUMOUS, 1950

"'Tis done," Rush wrote. "We have become a nation."

Catherine Drinker Bowen, *Miracle at Philadelphia,* 1966

The Martians stared back up at them for a long, long silent time
from the rippling water.

Ray Bradbury, *The Martian Chronicles,* 1950

I lingered round them, under that benign sky; watched the moth's
fluttering among the heath and hare's bells; listened to the soft wind

breathing through the grass; and wondered how any one could imagine unquiet slumbers for the sleepers in that quiet earth.

Emily Brontë, *Wuthering Heights,* **1847**

Across the chancel front above the pulpit was strung a crudely lettered banner: PEACE ON EARTH, GOOD WILL TO MEN.

Dee Brown, *Bury My Heart at Wounded Knee,* **1970**

—After all, he would not weep.

Pearl S. Buck, *Sons,* **1932**

"We are in Africa," said the dwarf.

Bartle Bull, *The White Rhino Hotel,* **1992**

Shall it be my lot to go that way again, I may give those that desire it an account of what I here am silent about; mean time I bid my reader *Adieu.*

John Bunyan, *The Pilgrim's Progress From This World to That Which Is to Come,* **PART 2, 1684**

I hoped there would be no dreams.

Anthony Burgess, *Earthly Powers,* **1980**

I have time for no more; the chaise now waits which is to conduct me to dear Berry Hill, and to the arms of the best of men.

Fanny Burney, *Evelina*, 1778

"I never knew who my father was."

Edgar Rice Burroughs, *Tarzan of the Apes*, 1914

"No good . . . no bueno . . . hustling myself"
                                        "No glot . . . C'lom Fliday"

William S. Burroughs, *Naked Lunch*, 1959

His father and grandfather could probably no more understand his state of mind than they could understand Chinese, but those who know him intimately do not know that they wish him greatly different from what he actually is.

Samuel Butler, *The Way of All Flesh*, POSTHUMOUS, 1903

Her Grace, too, had a sort of air rebuked—
Seemed pale and shivered, as if she had kept
A vigil, or dreamt rather more than slept.

Lord Byron, *Don Juan*, 1824

He knew what those jubilant crowds did not know but could have learned from books: that the plague bacillus never dies or disappears for good; that it can lie dormant for years and years in furniture and linen-chests; that it bides its time in bedrooms, cellars, trunks, and bookshelves; and that perhaps the day would come when, for the bane and the enlightening of men, it would rouse up its rats again and send them forth to die in a happy city.

Albert Camus, *The Plague*, 1947
Trans. by Stuart Gilbert, 1948

He felt like the salt marsh, the salt pond at high water, brimming.

John Casey, *Spartina*, 1990

Fortunate country, that is one day to receive hearts like Alexandra's into its bosom, to give them out again in the yellow wheat, in the rustling corn, in the shining eyes of youth!

Willa Cather, *O Pioneers!* 1913

"No, Uncle."

Louis-Ferdinand Céline, *Death on the Installment Plan*, 1936
Trans. by Ralph Manheim, 1966

"Farewell."

Miguel de Cervantes, *Don Quixote*, 1605
Trans. by John Ormsby, rev. by Joseph R. Jones, 1885

All they did was make me think of Silver-Wig, and I never saw
her again.

Raymond Chandler, *The Big Sleep*, 1939

It began to spot with rain.

Anton Chekhov, "The Duel," 1889
Trans. by Constance Garnett, n.d.

There was the hum of bees, and the musky odor of pinks filled
the air.

Kate Chopin, *The Awakening*, 1899

"Then," said Poirot, "having placed my solution before you, I have the honour to retire from the case. . . ."

Agatha Christie, *Murder on the Orient Express*, 1934

He vanished; I awoke from my dream.

Cicero, "The Dream of Scipio," *De re publica*, CA. 44 B.C.
Trans. by Joseph Pearl, 1968

But he would think of something.

Arthur C. Clarke, *2001: A Space Odyssey*, 1968

Ishido lingered three days and died very old.

James Clavell, *Shōgun*, 1975

I shall see you soon, and in the meantime think candidly of me, and believe me ever, Madam, Yours, &c., &c., &c.

John Cleland, *Fanny Hill*, 1749

He went like one that hath been stunned,
And is of sense forlorn:
A sadder and a wiser man,
He rose the morrow morn.

> **Samuel Taylor Coleridge,**
> *The Rime of the Ancient Mariner,* **1798**

Marian was the good angel of our lives—let Marian end our Story.

Wilkie Collins, *The Woman in White,* **1860**

Who can tell?

Wilkie Collins, *The Moonstone,* **1868**

"He feels it himself, and says often that he is, 'preparing to leave all this; preparing to leave . . .' while he waves his hand sadly at his butterflies."

Joseph Conrad, *Lord Jim,* **1900**

He passed on unsuspected and deadly, like a pest in the street full of men.

Joseph Conrad, *The Secret Agent,* **1907**

The cold air rushed against our faces.

Jack Conroy, *The Disinherited,* **1933**

In the morning I saw the sons of Unamis happy and strong; and yet, before the night has come, have I lived to see the last warrior of the wise race of the Mohicans.

James Fenimore Cooper, *The Last of the Mohicans,* **1826**

The only liberty taken by Middleton, was to add, "*May no wanton hand ever disturb his remains.*"

James Fenimore Cooper, *The Prairie,* **1827**

They did ordinary things that day, went to the playground, brought back a pizza, watched *The Muppets,* Billy went to bed, and Ted Kramer got to keep his son.

Avery Corman, *Kramer Versus Kramer,* **1977**

He turned now with a lover's thirst, to images of tranquil skies, fresh meadows, cool brooks; an existence of soft and eternal peace.

Stephen Crane, *The Red Badge of Courage*, 1895

His name lives in our ballads, our history, our hearts—so long as the English tongue is known.

Paul Creswick, *Robin Hood*, 1933

When at last he turned away, hastening for fear he should be late, there in the sky before him a bank of cloud lay brightly, bearing the shape of battlements.

A. J. Cronin, *The Citadel*, 1937

The guide and I entered by that hidden road to return into the bright world; and without caring for any rest,

we mounted up, he first, I second, so far that I distinguished through a round opening the beauteous things which Heaven bears; and thence we issued out, again to see the Stars.

Dante, "Hell", *The Divine Comedy,* **1300–15**
Trans. by John Aitken Carlyle, Thomas Okey, and P. H. Wickstead, 1950

Here power failed the high phantasy; but now my desire and will, like a wheel that spins with even motion, were revolved by the Love that moves the sun and the other stars.

Dante, "Paradise," *The Divine Comedy,* **1315–21**
Trans. by John D. Sinclair, 1946

And notwithstanding all the Fatigues and all the Miseries we have both gone thro', we are both in good Heart and Health; my husband remained there some time after me to settle our Affairs, and at first I had intended to go back to him, but at his desire I altered that Resolution, and he is to come over to *England* also, where we resolve to spend the Remainder of our years in sincere Penitence, for the wicked Lives we have lived.

Daniel Defoe, *Moll Flanders,* 1722

Holding Mike's hand, Auntie Mame drifted into the crowd, her sari floating out behind her.

Patrick Dennis, *Auntie Mame,* 1955

Such are the changes that a few years bring about, and so do things pass away, like a tale that is told!

Charles Dickens, *The Old Curiosity Shop,* 1840

And so, as Tiny Tim observed, God Bless Us, Every One!

Charles Dickens, *A Christmas Carol,* 1843

"It is a far, far better thing that I do, than I have ever done; it is a far, far better rest that I go to than I have ever known."

Charles Dickens, *A Tale of Two Cities,* 1859

And he slept.

Denis Diderot, *Jacques the Fatalist,* **1796**
Trans. by Michael Henry, 1986

The outline of the mountain was slowly smoothed and levelled out by the hand of distance.

Isak Dinesen, *Out of Africa,* **1937**

The claims of the Future are represented by suffering millions; and the Youth of a Nation are the trustees of Posterity.

Benjamin Disraeli, *Sybil; or, The Two Nations,* **1845**

And Harry K. Thaw, having obtained his release from the insane asylum, marched annually at Newport in the Armistice Day parade.

E. L. Doctorow, *Ragtime,* **1974**

Woodrow Wilson brought a bouquet of poppies.

John Dos Passos, *Nineteen Nineteen,* **1932**

That might be the subject of a new story, but our present story is ended.

Fyodor Dostoyevsky, *Crime and Punishment,* 1866
Trans. by Constance Garnett, 1934

"Mark my words, you'll see for yourself!" she concluded almost angrily, as she parted with Yevgeny Pavlovitch.

Fyodor Dostoyevsky, *The Idiot,* 1868
Trans. by Henry and Olga Carlisle, 1969

"And always so, all our lives hand in hand! Hurrah for Karamazov!" Kolya cried once more rapturously and once more all the boys chimed in.

Fyodor Dostoyevsky, *The Brothers Karamazov,* 1879–80
Trans. by Constance Garnett, rev. by Ralph E. Matlaw, 1976

"For me," said Sherlock Holmes, "there still remains the cocaine-bottle." And he stretched his long white hand up for it.

Sir Arthur Conan Doyle, *The Sign of Four,* 1890

"What's the use," he said wearily, as he stretched himself to rest.

Theodore Dreiser, *Sister Carrie,* **1900**

The small company, minus Russell, entered the yellow, unprepossessing door and disappeared.

Theodore Dreiser, *An American Tragedy,* **1925**

Thus in Thy good time may infinite reason turn the tangle straight, and these crooked marks on a fragile leaf be not indeed THE END.

W. E. B. Du Bois, *The Souls of Black Folk,* **1903**

Of the four valiant men whose history we have related, there now no longer remained but one single body; God had resumed the souls.

Alexandre Dumas, *The Man in the Iron Mask,* **1857**
Translator unknown

I leave this manuscript, I do not know for whom; I no longer know what it is about; stat rosa pristina nomine, nomina nuda tenemus.

Umberto Eco, *The Name of the Rose,* **1980**
Trans. by Warren Weaver, 1983

"Come in, Adam, and rest; it has been a hard day for thee."
George Eliot, *Adam Bede,* **1859**

In their death they were not divided.
George Eliot, *The Mill on the Floss,* **1860**

Chorus:
With joy, son of Atreus, sail on
To the Phrygian land,
With joy return,
Bringing glorious spoil from Troy.

Euripides, *Iphigenia in Aulis,* **405 B.C.**
Trans. by Charles R. Walker, 1958

And now as Robin's band beached itself and she bounded off and leaped toward me in search of accolades I looked directly at her—oh, I was as steady and steely-eyed as Lugosi—as though to say, tubby wimp or not, I shall in the end defeat you, Miss America, shall defeat you, learn to live with you, and make you mine.

Frederick Exley, *Last Notes From Home,* **1988**

A word that means the world to me.

James T. Farrell, *Judgment Day,* **1935**

And so long as men labored, and other men took and used the fruit of those who labored, the name of Spartacus would be remembered, whispered sometimes and shouted loud and clear at other times.

Howard Fast, *Spartacus,* **1951**

I dont hate it he thought, panting in the cold air, the iron New England dark; *I dont. I dont! I dont hate it! I dont hate it!*

William Faulkner, *Absalom, Absalom!* **1936**

"My receipt," Lucas said.

William Faulkner, *Intruder in the Dust,* **1948**

"There was hope."

Amanda Filipacchi, *Nude Men,* **1993**

"I know myself," he cried, "but that is all."

F. Scott Fitzgerald, *This Side of Paradise,* **1920**

And so we beat on, boats against the current, borne back ceaselessly into the past.

F. Scott Fitzgerald, *The Great Gatsby,* **1925**

Whether they lived happily ever after is not easily decided.

C. S. Forester, *The African Queen,* **1935**

The song died away; they heard the river, bearing down the snows of winter into the Mediterranean.

E. M. Forster, *A Room With a View,* **1908**

And somewhere the stinging smell of burning leaves.

John Fowles, *The Magus,* **1965**

I hold him to be the most amiable spirit who has ever flourished on the earth.

Anatole France, *The Romance of the Reine Pédauque,* **1893**
Translator unknown

Fifteen million men worked in the giant town.

Anatole France, *Penguin Island*, 1908
Trans. by Belle Notkin Burke

Let no pleasure tempt thee, no profit allure thee, no ambition corrupt thee, no example sway thee, no persuasion move thee, to do any thing which thou knowest to be evil; so shalt thou always live jollily; for a good conscience is a continual Christmas. Adieu.

Benjamin Franklin, *Poor Richard's Almanack*, 1733-58

The great green portal of the Ceballos mansion opened, and Jaime entered.

Carlos Fuentes, *The Good Conscience*, 1959
Trans. by Sam Hileman

The campaign was finally over.

Carlos Fuentes, *The Campaign*, 1990
Trans. by Alfred Mac Adam, 1991

He might wish and wish and never get it—the beauty and the loving in the world!

John Galsworthy, *To Let,* **1920**

Then he went into his house through the back door that had been open since six and fell on his face in the kitchen.

Gabriel García Márquez, *Chronicle of a Death Foretold,* **1981**
Trans. by Gregory Rabassa, 1981

"And now cover me up close, and let me go to sleep, and dream about my dear Cynthia, and my new shawl!"

Elizabeth Gaskell, *Wives and Daughters,* **1864**

I would like that line to portray Darling.

Jean Genet, *Our Lady of the Flowers,* **1943**
Trans. by Bernard Frechtman, 1963

It was among the ruins of the Capitol that I first conceived the idea of a work which has amused and exercised near twenty years of my life, and which, however inadequate to my own wishes, I finally deliver to the curiosity and candour of the public.

Edward Gibbon, *The History of the Decline and Fall of the Roman Empire*, 1776–88

There may be some truth in what she says. . . .

André Gide, *The Immoralist*, 1902
Trans. by Richard Howard, 1970

For he is an Englishman,
And he himself, has said it,
And its greatly to his credit
That he is an Englishman!

**Sir William Gilbert,
H.M.S. Pinafore, 1878**

O Gilgamesh, lord of Kullab, great is thy praise.

***Epic of Gilgamesh*, CA. 2000 B.C.**
Trans. by H. K. Sandars, 1960

"I am thankful to have finished with all that."

Ellen Glascow, *Barren Ground*, 1925

No clergyman attended.

Johann Wolfgang von Goethe, *The Sorrows of Young Werther*, 1774
Trans. by Elizabeth Mayer and Louise Bogan, 1971

Human discernment
Here is passed by;
Woman Eternal
Draws us on high.

Johann Wolfgang von Goethe,
***Faust*, part 2, 1831**
Trans. by Walter Arndt, 1976

"I invite you to examine your conscience more closely as well as the obligations of your earthly occupation, because that is something we can all picture to ourselves, and we are hardly . . ."

Nikolai Gogol, *Dead Souls*, 1842
Trans. by George Reavey, 1971

It now only remained that my gratitude in good fortune should exceed my former submission in adversity.

Oliver Goldsmith, *The Vicar of Wakefield,* **1766**

That autumn I went to Kazan in the secret hope that I might somehow manage to enrol as a student there.

Maksim Gorky, *My Apprenticeship,* **1915**
Trans. by Ronald Wilks, 1974

This was a base libel on Badger, who, though he cared little about Society, was rather fond of children; but it never failed to have its full effect.

Kenneth Grahame, *The Wind in the Willows,* **1908**

Each of us bathes by himself.

Günter Grass, *Dog Years,* **1963**
Trans. by Ralph Manheim, 1965

But everywhere he was kindly received, for the story of his life had become generally known.

Thomas Hardy, *The Return of the Native,* **1878**

"She's never found peace since she left his arms, and never will again till she's as he is now!"

Thomas Hardy, *Jude the Obscure,* **1895**

"I am reminded of that especially today when our troops will in foreseeable time be crossing the frontier."

Jaroslav Hašek, *The Good Soldier Švejk,* **1921–23**
Trans. by Cecil Parrott, 1973

"On a field, sable, the letter A, gules."

Nathaniel Hawthorne, *The Scarlet Letter,* **1850**

In the early morning on the lake sitting in the stern of the boat with his father rowing, he felt quite sure that he would never die.

Ernest Hemingway, "Indian Camp," 1924

"Yes," I said. "Isn't it pretty to think so?"

Ernest Hemingway, *The Sun Also Rises*, 1926

After a while I went out and left the hospital and walked back to the hotel in the rain.

Ernest Hemingway, *A Farewell to Arms*, 1929

The old man was dreaming about the lions.

Ernest Hemingway, *The Old Man and the Sea*, 1952

But this is how Paris was in the early days when we were very poor and very happy.

Ernest Hemingway, *A Moveable Feast*, 1964

The Persians had to admit that this was true and that Cyrus was wiser than they; so they left him, and chose rather to live in a rugged land and rule than to cultivate rich plains and be subject to others.

Herodotus, *The Histories*, CA. 446 B.C.
Trans. by Aubrey de Sélincourt, 1954

"Yes," he said, "eleven o'clock."
John Hersey, *A Bell for Adano,* **1944**

—Nu, what is the plan for tomorrow?
John Hersey, *The Wall,* **1950**

Pablo was waiting for me, and Mozart too.
Hermann Hesse, *Steppenwolf,* **1927**
Trans. by Basil Creighton, 1929

I turned and walked away through the rain.
Jack Higgins, *The Eagle Has Landed,* **1975**

This particular piece of evil was Navajo and the Navajos would have to pay for it.
Tony Hillerman, *A Thief of Time,* **1988**

"Do you think he will ever find it?" I asked.
James Hilton, *Lost Horizon,* **1933**

But Linford, at any rate, will remember and tell the tale: "I said good-bye to Chips the night before he died. . . ."

James Hilton, *Good-bye Mr. Chips,* **1934**

For such Truth, as opposeth no man's profit, nor pleasure, is to all men welcome.

Thomas Hobbes, *Leviathan,* **1651**

And so horse-taming Hector's rites gave up his soule to Rest.

Homer, *The Iliad,* CA. 9TH CENTURY B.C.
Trans. by George Chapman, completed 1611

> So they performed
> the funeral rites of Hektor, tamer of horses.
>
> *Trans. by Robert Fitzgerald, 1974*

Againe, then, twixt both parts the seed of Jove,
Athenian Pallas, of all future love
A league compos'd; and for her forme took choice
Of Mentor's likenesse both in Limb and Voice.

Homer, *The Odyssey,*
Trans. by George Chapman, 1616

A pact was sworn between the parts,
a treaty for all time: Athena's work
when she, the daughter of aegis-bearing Zeus,
had taken on lord Mentor's form and voice.

Trans. by Allen Mandelbaum, 1990

I kissed them one and all goodbye,
I said now don't you go and cry,
For I'll be homing by and by,
Oh, yes, father.

Paul Horgan, *A Distant Trumpet*, 1960

When they tried to release him from the skeleton he was embracing,
he crumbled into dust.

Victor Hugo, *Notre-Dame of Paris*, 1831
Trans. by John Sturrock, 1978

South-south-west, south, south-east, east. . . .

Aldous Huxley, *Brave New World*, 1932

Brack [*half-prostrate in the armchair*]: But, good God Almighty . . .
people don't do such things!

Henrik Ibsen, *Hedda Gabler,* 1890
Trans. by Jens Arup, 1966

But in the world according to Garp, we are all terminal cases.

John Irving, *The World According to Garp,* 1978

"Tell me, William," his last letter concluded, "*what* have I done to
deserve all this?"

Christopher Isherwood, *The Last of Mr. Norris,* 1935

"It isn't fair, it isn't right," Mrs. Hutchinson screamed, and then they were upon her.

Shirley Jackson, "The Lottery," 1948

It was to be feared that with the union, so far from brilliant, into which she was about to enter, these were not the last she was destined to shed.

Henry James, *The Bostonians*, 1886

But she turned to the door, and her headshake was now the end. "We shall never be again as we were!"

Henry James, *The Wings of the Dove*, 1902

His soul swooned slowly as he heard the snow falling faintly through the universe and faintly falling, like the descent of their last end, upon all the living and the dead.

James Joyce, "The Dead," *Dubliners,* **1914**

. . . or shall I wear red; yes and how he kissed me under the Moorish wall and I thought well as well him as another and then I asked him with my eyes to ask again yes and then he asked me would I yes to say yes my mountain flower and first I put my arms around him yes and drew him down to me so he could feel my breast all perfume yes and his heart was going like mad and yes I said yes I will Yes

James Joyce, *Ulysses,* **1922**

Away a lone a last a loved a long the

James Joyce, *Finnegans Wake,* **1939**

When he had nearly reached the lane, birds rose before him like an omen.

MacKinlay Kantor, *Andersonville,* **1955**

And it was as though he had said: Everything has begun.

Nikos Kazantzakis, *The Last Temptation of Christ,* **1951**
Trans. by P. A. Bien, 1960

I been away a long time.

Ken Kesey, *One Flew Over the Cuckoo's Nest,* **1962**

He crossed his hands on his lap and smiled, as a man may who has won salvation for himself and his beloved.

Rudyard Kipling, *Kim,* **1901**

It came from afar and travelled sedately on, a shrug of eternity.
   Arthur Koestler, *Darkness at Noon*, 1941
   Trans. by Daphne Hardy, 1941

She looked up through the water to find its source and caught sight of the tiny leaf that had touched her before.
   Jerzy Kosinski, *Steps*, 1968

"Horse Badorties is ready for the monsoon."
   William Kotzwinkle, *The Fan Man*, 1974

Happy Birthday Me.
   Larry Kramer, *Faggots*, 1978

That was the last thing he ever saw.
   Milan Kundera, *Life Is Elsewhere*, 1973
   Trans. by Peter Kussi, 1974

The strains of the piano and violin rose up weakly from below.
   Milan Kundera, *The Unbearable Lightness of Being*, 1984
   Trans. by Michael Henry Heim, 1984

I had, as usual, dismissed my maids before going to bed. . . .

Choderlos de Laclos, *Les Liaisons dangereuses,* **1782**
Trans. by P. W. K. Stone, 1961

If one could go deep into the depth of the dark earth one would discover "the bright gold," or if one could get fathoms down one would discover "the pearl at the bottom of the sea."

R. D. Laing, *The Divided Self,* **1960**

Then all found peace in a heap of livid dust.

Giuseppe di Lampedusa, *The Leopard,* **1958**
Trans. by Archibald Colquhoun, 1960

He walked towards the faintly humming, glowing town, quickly.

D. H. Lawrence, *Sons and Lovers,* **1913**

In the end he agreed, and then at once I knew how much I was sorry.

T. E. Lawrence, *Seven Pillars of Wisdom,* **1926**

Spying is waiting.

John le Carré, *The Russia House,* **1989**

Nothing more could I get out of him: he does not care generally for metaphysical discussion.

Mikhail Lermontov, *A Hero of Our Time,* **1940**
Trans. by Vladimir Nabokov with Dmitri Nabokov, 1958

It is no ordinary skeleton.

Gaston Leroux, *The Phantom of the Opera,* **1910**
Translator unknown

That newspaper bore the date of Tuesday 7 August 1945 and carried the news of the first atomic bomb, dropped on Hiroshima.

Primo Levi, *If Not Now, When?* **1982**
Trans. by William Weaver, 1985

The Japanese slipped forward with his camera, crouched, and took two three four pictures in quick succession.

Ira Levin, *Rosemary's Baby*, 1967

Sort of like in those old Hitler movies.

Ira Levin, *The Boys From Brazil*, 1976

"We shall yet make these United States a moral nation."

Sinclair Lewis, *Elmer Gantry*, 1927

How green was my Valley, then, and the Valley of them that have gone.

Richard Llewellyn, *How Green Was My Valley*, 1940

But if they have set limits to the duration of their legislative, and made this supreme power in any person or assembly only temporary; or else when, by the miscarriages of those in authority, it is forfeited; upon the forfeiture of their rulers, or at the determination of the time set, it reverts to the society, and the people have a right to act as supreme, and continue the legislative in themselves or place it in a new form, or new hands, as they think good.

John Locke, "An Essay Concerning the True Original, Extent and End of Civil Government," *Two Treatises of Government*, 1690

Philip shrugs. The camera stops, freezing him in mid-gesture.
   David Lodge, *Changing Places*, 1975

Come along—we'll just be in nice time for tea.
   Hugh Loftings, *The Voyages of Doctor Dolittle*, 1922

"And rescue us from ourselves," she completed, with a most adorable smile, whimsical as I had never seen it, for it was whimsical with love.
   Jack London, *The Sea-Wolf*, 1904

This passed away as the puppies' antics and mauling continued, and he lay with his half-shut, patient eyes, drowsing in the sun.
   Jack London, *White Fang*, 1906

Somebody threw a dead dog after him down the ravine.
   Malcolm Lowry, *Under the Volcano*, 1947

And when at last he was inside again he composed himself soberly to await the morning sun.

Carson McCullers, *The Heart Is a Lonely Hunter*, 1940

Still we do it.

Colleen McCullough, *The Thornbirds*, 1977

"Honey, never you mind. . . ."

Larry McMurtry, *The Last Picture Show*, 1966

"The woman," Dillard whispered. "The woman. They say he missed that whore."

Larry McMurtry, *Lonesome Dove*, 1985

When he entered, he heard Kamal's voice singing melodiously:

> *Visit me once each year,*
> *For it's wrong to abandon people forever.*

Naguib Mahfouz, *Palace Walk*, 1956
Trans. by William Maynard Hutchins and Olive E. Kenny, 1990

Hot dog!

Norman Mailer, *The Naked and the Dead*, 1948

"I hardly ever weep any more, now," she said with a bitter pride.

André Malraux, *Man's Fate*, 1933
Trans. by Harrison Smith and Robert Haas, Inc., 1934

It is not only the interest, but the duty of every individual, to use his utmost efforts to remove evil from himself, and from as large a circle as he can influence; and the more he exercises himself in his duty, the more wisely he directs his efforts, and the more successful these efforts are; the more he will probably improve and exalt his mind, and the more completely does he appear to fulfil the will of his Creator.

Thomas Robert Malthus, *An Essay on the Principle of Population As It Affects the Future Improvement of Society*, 1798

And before nightfall a shocked and respectful world received the news of his decease.

Thomas Mann, *Death in Venice*, 1911
Trans. by H. T. Lowe-Porter, 1930

But if we've succeeded in boring you instead, believe me, we didn't do it on purpose.

Alessandro Manzoni, *The Betrothed*, 1827
Trans. by Archibald Colquhoun, 1951

Pass on your way, then, with a smiling face, under the smile of him who bids you go.

Marcus Aurelius, *The Meditations*, CA. 180
Trans. by Maxwell Stallworth, 1964

George Apley died in his own house on Beacon Street on the thirteenth of December, 1933, two weeks after John Apley returned to Boston.

John P. Marquand, *The Late George Apley*, 1937

11. The philosophers have only *interpreted* the world, in various ways; the point, however, is to *change* it.

Karl Marx and Friedrich Engels, *Theses on Feuerbach*, **1888 [1845]**
Translator unknown, perhaps Samuel Moore

WORKING MEN OF ALL COUNTRIES, UNITE!

Karl Marx and Friedrich Engels, *The Communist Manifesto*, **1848**
Trans. by Samuel Moore, 1888

The only thing to be regretted is that the author of this book, great man as he is, has in recent years grown old and infirm with hoary frost upon his eyebrows.

Matsuo Bashō, *The Narrow Road to the Deep North*, **1689**
Trans. by Nobuyuki Yuasa, 1963

Cabs and omnibuses hurried to and fro, and crowds passed, hastening in every direction, and the sun was shining.

W. Somerset Maugham, *Of Human Bondage*, **1915**

He remembered the days when you could get thirteen Royal Natives for a shilling.

W. Somerset Maugham, *The Moon and Sixpence*, **1919**

"Have fun," she smiled. "It's Colombian."

Armistead Maupin, *Tales of the City*, 1978

I shall remain ignorant whether he succeeded in leaving the valley, or perished at the hands of the islanders.

Herman Melville, *Typee*, 1846

And thus, pursuers and pursued flew on, over an endless sea.

Herman Melville, *Mardi*, 1849

It was the devious-cruising Rachel, that in her retracing search after her missing children, only found another orphan.

Herman Melville, *Moby-Dick*, 1851

I am sleepy, and the oozy weeds about me twist.

Herman Melville, *Billy Budd, Foretopman*, POSTHUMOUS, 1924

But taking a glance at the others of her late company of actors, she compresses her lips.

George Meredith, *The Egoist*, 1879

Linda: . . . we're free . . . we're free . . .

Arthur Miller, *Death of a Salesman,* **1949**

The hills gently girdle it about: its course is fixed.

Henry Miller, *Tropic of Cancer,* **1934**

Commanders of power unequaled in human history, they have succeeded within the American system of organized irresponsibility.

C. Wright Mills, *The Power Elite,* **1956**

They looking back, all th' Eastern side beheld
Of Paradise, so late thir happie seat,
War'd over by that flaming Brand, the Gate
With dreadful Faces throng'd and fierie Armes:
Som natural tears they drop'd, but wip'd them soon;
The World was all before them, where to choose
Thir place of rest, and Providence thir guide:
They hand in hand with wandring steps and slow,
Through *Eden* took thir solitarie way.

John Milton, *Paradise Lost,* CA. **1667**

"After all, tomorrow is another day."

Margaret Mitchell, *Gone With the Wind,* **1936**

"'God's in his heaven, all's right with the world,'" whispered Anne softly.

L. M. Montgomery, *Anne of Green Gables,* **1908**

In the meane time, as I can not agree and consent to all thinges that he saide, beyng else without doubt a man singularly well learned, and also in all worldelye matters exactly and profoundly experienced, so much I nedes confesse and grant that many thinges be in the Utopian weale publique, whiche in our cities I maye rather wishe for, then hope after.

Sir Thomas More, *Utopia,* **1516**
Trans. by Ralphe Robynson, 1551

They smiled at each other slyly.

Christopher Morley, *The Haunted Bookshop,* **1919**

It was a fine cry—loud and long—but it had no bottom and it had no top, just circles and circles of sorrow.

Toni Morrison, *Sula,* **1973**

For now he knew what Shalimar knew: If you surrendered to the air, you could *ride* it.

Toni Morrison, *Song of Solomon,* **1977**

No one has ever been caught making love there again.

John Mortimer, *Titmuss Regained,* **1990**

His last view of her was standing alone in the big, empty hall with a bowl of chrysanthemums behind her.

Patricia Moyes, *Murder Fantastical,* **1967**

And this is the only immortality you and I may share, my Lolita.

Vladimir Nabokov, *Lolita,* **1955**

I cannot tell you what happened after this, except that knights and ladies, yes, and noble squires, too, were seen weeping there for the deaths of dear friends.

This story ends here:

> Such was
> The Nibelungs'
> Last Stand

The Nibelungenlied, CA. **1200**
Trans. by A. T. Hatto, 1965

He said, "What a marvelous summer. I think everybody knew it would be the last drop of pleasure."

Anaïs Nin, *Delta of Venus,* **1969**

A chill night breeze came whispering down from the depths of the valley, and suddenly the place was full of ghosts,—shadows of men alive and dead,—my own among them.

Charles Nordhoff and James Norman Hall, *Mutiny on the Bounty,* **1932**

The larger view always and through all shams, all wickednesses, discovers the Truth that will, in the end, prevail, and all things, surely, inevitably, resistlessly work together for good.

Frank Norris, *The Octopus,* **1901**

Ken's quick feet thudded across the Green, the gate rattled; and when the boy came running down the path, crying, "Oh, Flicka! Flicka!," the neigh that rang out on the cold air was a sound the filly had never made before.

Mary O'Hara, *My Friend Flicka,* **1941**

The creatures outside looked from pig to man, and from man to pig, and from pig to man again; but already it was impossible to say which was which.

George Orwell, *Animal Farm,* **1945**

He loved Big Brother.

George Orwell, *1984,* **1949**

It is important to kings and princes to be considered pious; and therefore they must confess themselves to you.

Blaise Pascal, *Pensées,* POSTHUMOUS, **1670**
Trans. by W. F. Trotter, 1904

And the book they held seemed to confirm and encourage their feeling.

Boris Pasternak, *Doctor Zhivago,* **1957**
Trans. by Manya Harari and Max Hayward, 1958

But when that dawn will come, of our emancipation, from the fear of bondage and the bondage of fear, why, that is a secret.

Alan Paton, *Cry, the Beloved Country,* **1948**

The eyes and the faces all turned themselves toward me, and guiding myself by them, as by a magical thread, I stepped into the room.

Sylvia Plath, *The Bell Jar,* **1963**

"So we shall be friend to ourselves and to the gods, both while we remain here and when, like victorious athletes who go about adding to their prizes, we receive the rewards of our justice, and in the journeys of a thousand years which I have described to you, we shall fare well."

Plato, *The Republic,* CA. 399 B.C.
Trans. by A. D. Lindsay, 1906

The hour of departure has arrived, and we go our ways—I to die, and you to live. Which is better God only knows.

Plato, *Apology,* CA. 399 B.C.
Trans. by Benjamin Jowett, 1928

Such was the end, Echecrates, of our friend, concerning whom I may truly say, that of all men of his time whom I have known, he was the wisest and justest and best.

Plato, *Phaedo,* CA. 399 B.C.
Trans. by Benjamin Jowett, 1928

The inquisition was in the hands of its enemies.

Edgar Allan Poe, "The Pit and the Pendulum," 1843

Then I walked back between the graves to the car and drove away.

Chaim Potok, *In the Beginning,* **1975**

But Flopsy, Mopsy, and Cotton-tail had bread and milk and blackberries for supper.

Beatrix Potter, *The Tale of Peter Rabbit*, 1900 [PRIVATELY PRINTED], 1902

The wind being favourable for Calais, I embarked for this port, and am now going to the house of one of my relations who lives a few miles off, where my brother said that he should anxiously await my arrival.

Abbé Prévost, *Manon Lescaut*, 1731
Trans. by D. C. Moylan, n.d.

Blessed is he who leaves the glory
Of life's gay feast ere time is up,
Who does not drain the brimming cup,
Nor reads the ending of the story,
But drops it without more ado,
As, my Onegin, I drop you.

Aleksandr Pushkin, *Eugene Onegin*, 1831
Trans. by Babette Deutsch, 1964

Now, everybody—

Thomas Pynchon, *Gravity's Rainbow*, 1973

Then there was only the ocean and the sky and the figure of Howard Roark.

Ayn Rand, *The Fountainhead,* **1943**

He raised his hand and over the desolate earth he traced in space the sign of the dollar.

Ayn Rand, *Atlas Shrugged,* **1957**

Somewhere beyond the sinkhole, past the magnolia, under the live oaks, a boy and a yearling ran side by side, and were gone forever.

Marjorie Kinnan Rawlings, *The Yearling,* **1938**

Turning him over one saw that he could not have suffered long; his face had an expression of calm, as though almost glad the end had come.

Erich Maria Remarque, *All Quiet on the Western Front,* **1928**
Trans. by A. W. Wheen, 1929

I lit the night-lamp and set it by the bed, and watched with him, till at morning the embalmers came to take him from me, and fill him with everlasting myrrh.

Mary Renault, *The Persian Boy,* **1972**

It was the hour between dog and wolf, as they say.

Jean Rhys, *After Leaving Mr. Mackenzie,* **1931**

"You see," he said, his voice filled with marvel. "You see."

Mordecai Richler, *The Apprenticeship of Duddy Kravitz,* **1959**

Destined to die in a country of strangers.

Conrad Richter, *A Country of Strangers,* **1966**

Should the counsel be guilty of improper conduct during the trial, the society can refuse to hear him, and can also punish him.

Henry Martyn Robert, *Robert's Rules of Order,* **1876**

Here ends the story that Turoldus tells.

Song of Roland, CA. **1130-70**
Trans. by Gerald J. Brault, 1978

ps. I dont care if I dont pass, I *love* the class.

Leo Rosten, *The Education of H∗y∗m∗a∗n K∗a∗p∗l∗a∗n*, 1937

I was back in plenty of time for work.

Philip Roth, "Goodbye, Columbus," 1959

"It's like being married to Tolstoy," he said, and left me to make my feverish notes while he started off after the runaway spouse, some five minutes now into her doomed journey in search of a less noble calling.

Philip Roth, *The Ghost Writer*, 1979

But all this forms a new subject that is far too vast for my narrow scope. I ought throughout to have kept to a more limited sphere.

Jean Jacques Rousseau, *The Social Contract*, 1762
Trans. by G. D. H. Cole, 1913

Perhaps they could all go to have dinner at the Hazeltines.

Robert Ruark, *The Honey Badger*, 1965

"I'm coming," he answered her, and turned away from the view.

Salman Rushdie, *The Satanic Verses*, 1988

Francesca sat in stricken silence, crushing the folded morsel of paper tightly in her hand and wondering if the thin, cheerful voice with its pitiless, ghastly mockery of consolation would never stop.

Saki, *The Unbearable Bassington*, 1912

Her lips began to move, forming soundless words, and they continued to move.

J. D. Salinger, "Franny," 1955

For some minutes, before she fell into a deep, dreamless sleep, she just lay quiet, smiling at the ceiling.

J. D. Salinger, "Zooey," 1957

And the following day the banns were announced for the marriage of Pierre André and Marianne Chevreuse.

George Sand, *Marianne*, 1876
Trans. by Siân Miles, 1987

The prairie years, the war years, were over.

Carl Sandburg, *Abraham Lincoln: The War Years,* **1939**

Sick to death, she nevertheless smiled at the soldier, and said, "Won't you please come in and let me show you around the house?"

William Saroyan, *The Human Comedy,* **1943**

"My God! I don't know what's come to this Club."

Dorothy L. Sayers, *The Unpleasantness at the Bellona Club,* **1928**

And some day I would like to see it published, as a blueprint of a way of life that was paying dividends in America in the first half of the twentieth century.

Budd Schulberg, *What Makes Sammy Run?* **1941**

His fate was destined to a foreign strand,
A petty fortress and an "humble" hand;
He left the name at which the world grew pale,
To point a moral or adorn a TALE.

Sir Walter Scott, *Ivanhoe,* **1819**

"You know," I said, "I think this is going to be fun."

Carolyn See, *Rhine Maidens,* **1981**

And to say goodbye.

Erich Segal, *The Class,* **1985**

All of us felt how ruthlessly and fearfully outward powers could strike to the very core of man, but at the same time we felt that at the very core there was something that was unassailable and inviolable.

Anna Seghers, *The Seventh Cross,* **1942**
Trans. by James A. Galston, 1943

> *Bolingbroke:*
> March sadly after; grace my mourning here,
> In weeping after this untimely bier.

William Shakespeare, *Richard the Second,* **1595**

> *Puck:*
> Give me your hands, if we be friends,
> And Robin shall restore amends.

William Shakespeare, *A Midsummer Night's Dream,* **1595-96**

Fortinbras:
Take up the bodies. Such a sight as this
Becomes the field, but here shows much amiss.
Go bid the soldiers shoot.

William Shakespeare, *Hamlet*, 1600

Edgar:
The oldest hath borne most; we that are young
Shall never see so much, nor live so long.

William Shakespeare, *King Lear*, 1605–06

Malcolm:
So thanks to all at once and to each one,
Whom we invite to see us crowned at Scone.

William Shakespeare, *Macbeth*, CA. 1606

Michael watched her walk, thinking what a pretty gal, what nice legs.

Irwin Shaw, "The Girls in Their Summer Dresses," 1939

He was soon borne away by the waves and lost in darkness and distance.

Mary Shelley, *Frankenstein; or, The Modern Prometheus*, 1818

Lady Teagle:
"No more in vice or error to engage,
Or play the fool at large on life's great stage."

**Richard Brindsley Sheridan,
The School for Scandal, 1777**

And again after a little while, under the mound, right by the shrine, in the shaggy shelter of the old wormwood, a female bustard laid nine speckled, smoky-blue eggs and sat on them, warming them with her body, protecting them with her glossy wings.

Mikhail Sholokhov, *And Quiet Flows the Don*, 1928
Trans. by Stephen Garry, 1934

Then she put the tablets in her mouth and swallowed them down with a mouthful of brandy, sitting behind the wheel of her big car.

Nevil Shute, *On the Beach*, 1957

"CHICAGO WILL BE OURS!"
Upton Sinclair, *The Jungle*, 1906

She closed the windows.
Betty Smith, *A Tree Grows in Brooklyn*, 1943

Before he departed, the knight made him partake of his bounty, though he could not make him taste of his happiness, which soon received a considerable addition in the birth of a son, destined to be the heir and representative of two worthy families, whose mutual animosity, the union of his parents had so happily extinguished.
Tobias Smollett, *The Life and Adventures of Sir Launcelot Greaves*, 1761

It was a homecoming such as I had imagined when I was lonely, but as one happening to others, not to me.
C. P. Snow, *Homecoming*, 1956

The movement for social revolution in China might suffer defeats, might temporarily retreat, might for a time languish, might make wide changes in tactics to fit immediate necessities and aims, might even for a period be submerged, be forced underground, but it would not only continue to mature; in one mutation or another it would eventually win, simply because (as this book proves, if it proves anything) the basic conditions which had given it birth carried within themselves the dynamic necessity for its triumph.

Edgar Snow, *Red Star Over China,* **1938**

"One can only conclude that the provisioning of the capital is excellent."

Aleksandr I. Solzhenitsyn, *The First Circle,* **1968**
Trans. by Thomas P. Whitney, 1968

Damn them all.

Susan Sontag, *The Volcano Lover,* **1992**

And now for this last time, Jade, I don't mind, or even ask if it is madness: I see your face, I see you; I see you in every seat.

Scott Spencer, *Endless Love,* **1979**

"I am afraid it comes very near being a dead-lock," she groaned, dropping her head on her arms.

Gertrude Stein, *Three Lives,* **1909**

She did not attempt to take her own life in any way; but, with her children in her arms, she died three days after Julian.

Stendhal, *The Red and the Black,* **1830**
Trans. by Lowell Bair, 1958

So that when I stretched out my hand, I caught hold of the fille de chambre's ———

Laurence Sterne, *A Sentimental Journey,* **1768**

Here, then, as I lay down the pen, and proceed to seal up my confession, I bring the life of that unhappy Henry Jekyll to an end.

Robert Louis Stevenson, *The Strange Case of Dr. Jekyll and Mr. Hyde,* **1886**

If I concern myself for myself, the unique one, then my concern rests on its transitory, mortal creator, who consumes himself, and I may say: All things are nothing to me.

Max Stirner, *The Ego and His Own,* **1844**
Trans by Steven T. Byington, 1907

We had great reason to thank God who had spared us.

Bram Stoker, *Dracula*, 1897

He felt his soul would leave his body, rise upward into the dome, becoming part of it: part of space, of time, of heaven, and of God.

Irving Stone, *The Agony and the Ecstasy*, 1961

A man has nothing to fear, he thought to himself, who understands history.

Robert Stone, *A Flag for Sunrise*, 1981

Another blast from the whistle, a roar, a gigantic sound; and it seemed to soar into the dusk beyond and above them forever, with a noise, perhaps, like the clatter of the opening of everlasting gates and doors—passed swiftly on—toward Richmond, the North, the oncoming night.

William Styron, *Lie Down in Darkness*, 1951

"Deed it does," he said.

William Styron, *The Long March*, 1952

Morning: excellent and fair.

William Styron, *Sophie's Choice,* **1979**

Domitian himself, it is said, dreamed that a golden hump grew out on his back, and he regarded this as an infallible sign that the condition of the empire would be happier and more prosperous after his time; and this was shortly shown to be true through the uprightness and moderate rule of the succeeding emperors.

Suetonius, *Lives of the Caesars,* CA. **122**
Trans. by J. C. Rolfe, 1913

I dwell the longer upon this Subject from the Desire I have to make the Society of an *English Yahoo* by an Means not insupportable; and therefore I here intreat those who have any Tincture of this absurd Vice, that they will not presume to appear in my Sight.

Jonathan Swift, *Gulliver's Travels,* **1726**

His bride-to-be was gone.
   Booth Tarkington, *Seventeen,* **1916**

Her eyes would look wistful no more.
   Booth Tarkington, *The Magnificent Ambersons,* **1918**

I watched his back receding down the long, gleaming hall.
   Donna Tartt, *The Secret History,* **1992**

> The goal of this great world
> Lies beyond sight; yet—if our slowly-grown
> And crown'd Republic's crowning common sense,
> That saved her many times, not fail—their fears
> Are morning shadows huger than the shapes
> That cast them, not those gloomier which forego
> The darkness of that battle in the west
> Where all of high and holy dies away.
>
>   **Alfred, Lord Tennyson,** *Idylls of the King,* **1859–85**

What a most extraordinary idea.

Josephine Tey, *The Singing Sands*, 1952

—Come, children, let us shut up the box and the puppets, for our play is played out.

William Makepeace Thackeray, *Vanity Fair*, 1848

Then, with the faint, fleeting smile playing around his lips, he faced the firing squad; erect and motionless, proud and disdainful, Walter Mitty the Undefeated, inscrutable to the last.

James Thurber, "The Secret Life of Walter Mitty," 1939

"Well, I'm back," he said.

J. R. R. Tolkien, *The Return of the King*, 1955

He drew in a breath, broke off in the middle of it, stretched himself out, and died.

Leo Tolstoy, *The Death of Ivan Ilyich*, 1864–69
Trans. by Lynn Solotaroff, 1981

In the first case, it was necessary to renounce the recognition of a non-existent immovability in space and recognize the motion which is imperceptible to our own senses; even so, in the present case, it is necessary to renounce the non-existent freedom and recognize the dependence of which we are not conscious.

Leo Tolstoy, *War and Peace,* **1864–69**
Trans. by Leo Wiener, 1904

Taking the pigtail in one of his paws, he pressed it warmly to his wet moustache.

John Kennedy Toole, *A Confederacy of Dunces,* **1980**

Gold-glowing child, it steps into the sky and sends a birth-song slanting down the gray dust streets and sleepy windows of the southern town.

Jean Toomer, *Cane,* **1923**

No sooner was he seated in the saddle than the Indians shouted, whipped their ponies into action, and hurried back home.

B. Traven, *The Treasure of the Sierra Madre,* **1927**
Trans. by author, 1937

When the season's over I walk among the shrubs myself, making the most of the colors while they last and the fountain while it flows.

William Trevor, *My House in Umbria,* **1991**

There is the funeral, and then the lovers die together.

William Trevor, *Reading Turgenev,* **1991**

I remained alone, completely alone, between two immensities, the sea and the sky.

Flora Tristan, *Peregrinations of a Pariah,* **1838**

He knows the way, however, to Boxall Hall as well as ever he did, and is willing to acknowledge, that the tea there is almost as good as it ever was at Greshamsbury.

Anthony Trollope, *Doctor Thorne,* **1858**

Thus once again would the will of Catherine the Great be accomplished.

Henri Troyat, *Catherine the Great,* **1977**
Trans. by Joan Pinkham, 1980

The nations were caught in a trap, a trap made during the first thirty days out of battles that failed to be decisive, a trap from which there was, and has been, no exit.

Barbara W. Tuchman, *The Guns of August,* **1962**

However passionate, sinning, and rebellious the heart hidden in that tomb, the flowers growing over it peep serenely at us with their innocent eyes; they tell us not of eternal peace alone, of that great peace of the "indifferent" nature; they tell us, too, of eternal reconciliation and of life without end.

Ivan Turgenev, *Fathers and Sons,* **1862**
Trans. by Constance Garnett, rev. by Ralph E. Matlaw, 1972

. . . About two in the morning he returned to his study.

Ivan Turgenev, *Spring Torrents,* **1872**
Trans. by Leonard Shapiro, 1972

Some day it may seem worth while to take up the story of the younger ones again, and see what sort of men and women they turned out to be; therefore it will be wisest not to reveal any of that part of their lives at present.

Mark Twain, *The Adventures of Tom Sawyer,* **1876**

The Pennsylvania road rushed us to New York without missing schedule ten minutes anywhere on the route; and there ended one of the most enjoyable five-thousand-mile journeys I have ever had the good fortune to make.

Mark Twain, *Life on the Mississippi,* **1883**

But I reckon I got to light out for the Territory ahead of the rest, because Aunt Sally she's going to adopt me and sivilize me, and I can't stand it. I been there before.

Mark Twain, *The Adventures of Huckleberry Finn,* **1884**

They were so bright and festive, for a moment he thought they were confetti.

Anne Tyler, *The Accidental Tourist,* **1985**

Another nail in his coffin. His.
John Updike, *Rabbit Is Rich*, 1981

"You can pay for my drinks. I'm flat broke."
Mario Vargas Llosa, *The Time of the Hero*, 1962
Trans. by Lysander Kemp, 1966

"They'll find a way, you'll see!"
Jules Verne, *From the Earth to the Moon*, 1865
Trans. by Lowell Bair, 1967

Truly, would you not for less than that make the tour around the world?

Jules Verne, *Around the World in Eighty Days*, 1873
Trans. by George M. Towle, 1873

Go little she-goats, Hesper comes, go home replete.

Virgil, *The Eclogues*, 40 B.C.
Trans. by Guy Lee, 1980

—That is very well put, said Candide, but we must cultivate our garden.

Voltaire, *Candide*, 1759
Trans. by Robert M. Adams, 1966

One bird said to Billy Pilgrim, *"Poo-tee-weet?"*

Kurt Vonnegut, *Slaughterhouse-Five*, 1969

Amen.

Alice Walker, *The Color Purple*, 1982

I thank my daughter Rebecca for giving me the opportunity to be a mother.

Alice Walker, *Possessing the Secret of Joy*, 1992

"You're looking unusually cheerful to-day," said the second-in-command.

Evelyn Waugh, *Brideshead Revisited*, 1944

They were there in the forest at the hour of death.

Jiri Weil, *Mendelssohn Is on the Roof*, 1960
Trans. by Marie Winn, 1991

They heard through falling rain the running of the horse and bear, the stroke of the leopard, the dragon's crusty slither, and the glimmer and the trumpet of the swan.

Eudora Welty, "The Wanderers," *The Golden Apples,* **1949**

His son's cross lay upon his heart.

Franz Werfel, *The Forty Days of Musa Dagh,* **1933**
Trans. by Geoffrey Dunlop, 1934

There was a knock on the door, and they delayed only long enough to smile at each other, and to exchange a kiss.

Rebecca West, *The Birds Fall Down,* **1966**

He knelt by the bed and bent over her, draining their last moment to its lees; and in the silence there passed between them the word which made all clear.

Edith Wharton, *The House of Mirth,* **1905**

At that, as if it had been the signal he waited for, Newland Archer got up slowly and walked back alone to his hotel.

Edith Wharton, *The Age of Innocence,* **1920**

Perhaps indeed the efforts of the true poets, founders, religions, literatures, all ages, have been, and ever will be, our time and times to come, essentially the same—to bring people back from their persistent strayings and sickly abstractions, to the costless average, divine, original concrete.

Walt Whitman, *Specimen Days,* **1882**

The look in his eyes, as they stared into mine, has never left me.

Elie Wiesel, *Night,* **1956**
Trans. by Stella Rodway

It was not till they had examined the rings that they recognized who it was.

Oscar Wilde, *The Picture of Dorian Gray,* **1891**

Herod: Kill that woman.

Oscar Wilde, *Salomé,* **1894**

Perhaps I am chosen to teach you something much more wonderful, the meaning of Sorrow, and its beauty. Your affectionate friend Oscar Wilde

Oscar Wilde, *De Profundis*, 1905

"There is a land of the living and a land of the dead and the bridge is love, the only survival, the only meaning."

Thornton Wilder, *The Bridge of San Luis Rey*, 1927

Whereof one cannot speak, thereof one must be silent.

Ludwig Wittgenstein, *Tractatus Logico-Philosophicus*, 1921
Trans. by C. K. Ogden, 1922

"Not at all, sir."

P. G. Wodehouse, *Thank You, Jeeves*, 1934

"—Whereon the pillars of this earth are founded, toward which the conscience of the world is tending—a wind is rising, and the rivers flow."

Thomas Wolfe, *You Can't Go Home Again*, 1940

The bus was there, parked beside the Space Heater House.
   Tom Wolfe, *The Electric Kool-Aid Acid Test,* **1968**

Yes, she thought, laying down her brush in extreme fatigue, I have had my vision.
   Virginia Woolf, *To the Lighthouse,* **1927**

You had to remind this man that he loved his wife.
   Herman Wouk, *The Winds of War,* **1971**

He heard the ring of steel against steel as a far door clanged shut.
   Richard Wright, *Native Son,* **1940**

Like thee, may New Switzerland flourish and prosper—good, happy, and free!
   Johann Wyss, *The Swiss Family Robinson,* **1813**
   Trans. by William H. G. Kingston

To Berlin! To Berlin! To Berlin!

Emile Zola, *Nana*, 1880
Trans. by George Holden, 1972

Men were springing forth, a black avenging army, germinating slowly in the furrows, growing towards the harvests of the next century, and their germination would soon overturn the earth.

Emile Zola, *Germinal*, 1885
Trans. by Havelock Ellis, 1925

Here was the Dead, there was the Seed; and bread would be springing from the Good Earth.

Emile Zola, *La Terre*, 1888
Trans. by Douglas Parmée, 1980

Acknowledgments

To my many friends whose suggestions of suitable first and last lines were invaluable in the making of this book.

Acknowledgment must also go to those who were generous with their facilities and time. Foremost is Hasan Wazani and his associate, John Schreiner, of the wonderful Discount Bookstore in New York City. Also most considerate was Doubleday's Fifth Avenue flagship store. Equally helpful were the various Dutchess County, N.Y., libraries: Millbrook, Rhinebeck, Stanfordville, and Pine Plains, as well as the Vassar College collection.

The author trusts he was not too obstructive of aisles, nor too guilty of misshelving books.

Index

❧❧❧❧